Imperfect

....

Colette Rommis

Copyright © 2023 by Colette Rommis

All rights reserved.

No portion of this book may be reproduced in any form without written permission from the publisher or author, except as permitted by U.S. copyright law.

Contents

Prologue	1
Chapter 1	7
Chapter 2	37
Chapter 3	62
Chapter 4	99
Chapter 5	131
Chapter 6	161
Chapter 7	195
Chapter 8	221
Chapter 9	241

Contents

Prologue	1
Chapter 1	7
Chapter 2	37
Chapter 3	62
Chapter 4	99
Chapter 5	131
Chapter 6	161
Chapter 7	195
Chapter 8	221
Chapter 9	241

Prologue

Prologue

I couldn't remember my address.

33...5? Was it five or was it six? It was definitely three three...something...wasn't it?

Yes, there were two threes because my sister was three and if there were two Paige's then that would be the beginning of my address and then it was a...six, right? Because I was six. Two Paige's and one Nell made the address of my home.

Only...

I just turned six. Did I remember my address before or after my birthday?

My lower lip started to shake and my eyes started to burn, like I was going to cry as I tried to look for my mother. Where was she? "Mom?" I called out, my voice sounding small, the noise of the crowd making it hard for even me to hear it.

We're going shopping. C'mon Nell, just you and me.

I was at the mall with my mom and she'd wanted something extra special so we were driving for a long time before we stopped. I didn't know where I was but it was okay because I was holding mommy's hand.

I looked down at my empty hand, a teardrop landing right in the middle of it.

I let her go.

I let go of her hand and now I was lost and I couldn't remember my address.

"Mommy?" I said, my voice even quieter than last time, no one even pausing as they walked by me, some of them bumping into me until my back was pressed against the wall, my eyes scanning the people with big bags as they rushed by.

I started to cry harder, my tears falling faster, my legs shaking so hard that I couldn't stand straight anymore and I let myself sink to the ground, my butt hitting the floor hard.

She'd been holding my hand and then I'd seen a stuffed animal in the window of a shop. It was a dog, so big that my arms wouldn't even wrap around him and before I knew it, my face had been pressed up against the glass, my hand no longer holding my mom's, my eyes locked on that dog as I'd asked her if I could have him.

But she hadn't answered.

She didn't answer when I asked again and when I turned around...

She was gone.

"Mom!" I tried to shout but my throat felt tight and it felt like an elastic band was wrapped around my chest. The sound of Jingle Bells was much louder than the small noise I'd made. No one noticed me.

I buried my face in my hands, pulling my knees up to my chest, my brain spinning as I tried to remember what I was supposed to do if I ever got lost.

"Are you okay, sweetie?"

I blinked, pulling my face from my hands to raise my head and look at the woman crouched in front of me. She was smiling at me, her eyes crinkled at the corners as she reached her hand out to give my knee a pat.

I shook my head as I started to cry harder.

"Are you lost?"

I nodded, unable to speak because of the elastic band around my chest.

"C'mon," she said, holding out her hand for me to take. "Let's go find your parents, okay?"

The pain in my chest eased as I placed my hand in the woman's, remembering that the first thing I needed to do when I got lost was to get help.

"What's your name, sweetheart?" the woman asked as she helped me stand up.

"Penelope," I said, sniffling.

"That's a pretty name," she said, giving me a warm smile.

"T-thank you," I stuttered, not wanting to argue with her even though I didn't really like my name. The other kids at school made fun of me, telling me it was weird.

"What about your last name?" Her voice was soft, like my teacher's, her eyes were calm and her hand was warm and I felt myself relaxing as we began to move through the crowd.

"Watson."

"Okay, Penelope Watson, we're going to get you home, alright?"

I started to feel better but for some reason I started to cry harder and then the woman's arms were wrapped around me, tugging me close to her. She was so warm so I wrapped my small arms around her neck, holding tight. She'd stopped for me when no one else had.

"Get your hands off of my daughter."

I looked up quickly to see my mother walking towards us, her pretty blue eyes had that look in them that they got when I was in trouble, her hands were on her hips and her mouth was doing that thing where it turned down a little in the corners.

"Mommy!" I yelled, struggling to get out of the woman's hold and she let me go immediately. I ran to my mother and flung my arms around her, pressing my face into her stomach, the pressure in my chest going away entirely.

"I...thought she was lost," the other woman said, her voice a little less warm now but I didn't care. My mom had found me! It didn't matter that I couldn't remember my address, my mom had found me!

"Well, she's not," my mother snapped, using her angry voice.

"Um, okay, that's good," the other woman mumbled before joining the rest of the fast moving crowd and disappearing.

"I was scared," I said, my tears renewing their force, this time in relief as I pressed myself closer to my mom, never wanting to let her go.

She pressed her hands into my shoulders, forcing me to release my grip before she knelt down in front of me and gripped my arms hard enough to make me wince. When our faces were level, my tears began to slow and

I felt my heart do an odd flip inside of me as I saw the expression on her face.

Was she mad at me? I didn't mean to let her go. Couldn't she see that it was an accident?

"You let go of my hand, Nell. What were you thinking?" She gave me a slight shake, her fingers digging into my arms a bit harder.

"I-I'm sorry," I said, my voice cracking.

"I know you are but that doesn't change the fact that you were a very bad girl. Your father will be angry about this, Nell."

My lip started to tremble and I started to cry again. "He will?"

"Of course." She sighed and gave me a hard look before saying, "We don't have to tell him."

I brightened and nodded my head eagerly. I hated it when my daddy was mad at me.

"Okay, I promise not to tell him as long as you promise you'll never tell him either." I nodded but her eyes hardened and she gave me another shake, making my teeth click together. "Promise me, Nell," she said, her voice sharp, making me wince.

"I promise," I whispered.

Finally, she nodded and scooped me up into her arms, planting me on her hip as we walked through the mall.

I wrapped my arms around her neck, just like I'd done to the stranger earlier and I fleetingly thought that she'd been a little warmer than my mommy, her skin just a tad softer.

I shook off the thought, tightening my arms, not caring how warm or cold she was, as long as I had my mommy back.

Chapter 1

Right right, meant to tell you guys, just wanted to post something new so that when She's Bad News is done, you'll have something to read. Let me know what you think. I found this super hard to write. I'll be working on SBN now.

Shaboopie.

Chapter 1

Funny how you could miss someone even though they were right next to you.

At this moment, I missed my sister.

I missed her so much that it hurt, that it made my chest literally ache from the pressure of it.

"God, you're so dumb."

I closed my eyes, trying to erase the image of her face at that moment. Her full lips were curled into a sneer, her straight nose a little higher than usual so that she could look down it at me with her too familiar eyes. It was her eyes that hurt the most. She had gorgeous blue eyes with flecks of grey in them. They were one feature we almost shared. Those flecks of grey matched the exact shade of my own eyes and ever since she was born, I felt like I was part of her in a way that could never be taken from us. From the moment she was born, it was Paige and Nell against the world.

Only Paige didn't feel like that anymore.

"When are you going to stop following me around like a little puppy?" Paige shrieked.

Hey Nell, let's sneak out and watch the stars.

I flinched when I felt her fingers wrap around my arm, her manicured nails cutting into the skin exposed by my white t-shirt.

"Look at me," she hissed, her voice close to my ear. I would've traded anything to disappear right then, to not have to look at my baby sister and see the hate in her eyes.

Instead, I took a long, deep breath and did as she asked, opening my eyes and turning my head towards her.

And there it was.

Hate.

Vicious and poignant, steady and so solid that I felt like I could reach out and touch it.

Or maybe it was the other way around. It was her hate that could touch me, that could brush up against me and leave a mark just under my skin like a scar.

"Did I ask you to come here?" she snarled, her breath smelling of mint and whiskey, her voice just a bit slurred. "Did I call and beg for a ride from my responsible big sister? No?" She gave me a humourless grin tinged with a cruelty that made something inside of me twist painfully. "Then did someone invite you here? Did anyone else at this party call you up and say, 'Hey Nell, you should come out'?" Her smile widened a second before she tilted her head back and laughed hard. At me.

"Stop it," I whispered, my throat clogging with unshed tears, pressure building behind my eyelids and at my temples as I raised a hand to wrap my fingers around her wrist, trying to get her to loosen her grip. "I'll leave, okay, just let me go."

"Hey guys!" she shouted instead, her gaze brushing over me as she addressed the rest of the party, the thumping music drowning out her voice but those close enough to hear stopped to give her their attention. "Did you invite this girl?" A few of them laughed and every single one of them shook their head, confirming what we all already knew. "See?" Paige said, looking back down at me, the cruelty in her eyes hitting me harder than any punch. "You're not welcome here." She leaned in closer to me, her heels making her a half an inch taller than me as she whispered, her voice suddenly slur free and steady. "Now fuck off, Nell."

Why are you crying, Nellie?

"Yeah," I whispered, my heart in my throat, the pounding music pressing on my skull, making my head ache so badly that I thought it might explode.

I needed to get out of there.

I hate it when you cry.

I pulled at my arm too hard, having not been prepared for Paige's grip to no longer be there. She'd already released me so when I'd yanked, my arm shot out and hit the person next to me causing her drink to spill.

All over her friend.

"Watch it, bitch!" the girl who'd received the brunt of the drink yelled at me, her overly made up face contorted in fury as she held her arms away from her body, gripping her dripping shirt with the tips of her fingers.

"Sorry," I mumbled, feeling my throat close as my heart started beating faster, demanding air.

Why was it so hot in there?

My breath wheezed in and out of my lungs as I lurched forward, pressing between people, spilling more drinks in the process but not caring. Where was the fucking door?

My skin was covered in a fine sheen of sweat and my palms were starting to itch in that familiar, uncomfortable way when I finally found the door and burst through it, startling the group of people standing outside, smoking a joint.

"What's her problem?" One of the girls said as I brushed past them, my steps shaky, my breathing frantic as I sucked in giant pulls of the cool, night air.

I hated crowds. They did something to me, sucked all the air out of my lungs, made my skin feel too tight until I felt like I was going to burst out of it.

I was just starting to feel a little calmer when Brian, Paige's boyfriend appeared in front of me.

"Hey Nell," Brian said, his mouth curled up in one corner, the other corner holding a cigarette between his lips. "I didn't know you were here."

I sucked in a shaking breath and narrowed my eyes at him, hating the way his golden hair had just the right amount of curl, the way his broad shoulders filled out the sweater he was wearing to perfection. He was tall and his build was just the right mix of lean and muscular. He'd been a star football player the year before, destined for the NFL draft until he'd blown his knee. Now he could barely run, all his dreams had been crushed and everything had changed for him.

He'd been a decent guy before. The guy who'd met Paige, who made her fall in love with him, had been all right. He'd never smoked, rarely drank and steered clear of drugs, always conscious of what it could mean to his future if he got caught.

Then it didn't matter anymore.

Now he dragged my sister to places like this, places that were miles away from our side of town, places where the rougher crowds tended to hang out.

"You brought my sister to this place," I said, my voice shaking and my fingers curling in until my nails were digging into my palms.

He pulled the cigarette out of his mouth and released a long breath of smoky air into the night. "Relax Nell," he said, flashing his charming grin that now had that edge of anger that never seemed to go away. He was pissed at me, at the cigarette in his hand, at his injury, at the world.

He couldn't see past it, didn't care to and because Paige loved him...

She'd follow him anywhere.

"She's a big girl. It was her choice to come with me," he said, giving a careless shrug, taking another pull on his cigarette before leaning in close and blowing smoke into my face as he whispered, "Loosen up, Nell. She's having fun and my guess is you already asked her to leave and she refused. Why don't you just go home and do your homework like you usually do on Friday nights, okay?" His lips twisted into a mocking grin, the laughter in his eyes making my teeth grit in anger.

He was laughing at me. Just like Paige had, just like everyone in my family did.

"It's just a party. You didn't have to take time out of your busy schedule to come all the way over here." He snorted, cocking his head to the side as he looked at me. "Did you think she'd see you as some big hero? That she'd be happy to go home with you, thankful that you dragged her away from a good time?"

My fists started to shake at my sides. "I saw someone doing coke in there, Brian. This isn't her kind of party."

"How would you know what kind of parties your sister likes to go to? You don't even know her."

I used to. I used to know her better than anyone.

And she never used to look at me like she had tonight.

My chest ached at the memory, hating that everything had changed, hating that they'd gotten to her, the one person in the world I thought I could trust.

"Yeah," I whispered, half turning my body away from Brian, ready to go, ready to forget about this night and all the stupid thoughts that had been going through my head when I'd come here. I wanted to talk to her, to clear everything up and instead...

I'd just confirmed that she hated me.

"Just...don't leave her alone in there, okay?"

I turned to leave, my throat clogging with everything I was desperately trying to keep inside, to ignore until it just went away.

I'd barely taken a step when Brian's hand was wrapped around my forearm, tugging me until I stumbled into him, our bodies suddenly chest to chest.

"What's the matter, Nell?" he hissed, his face contorted in fury, his eyes blood-shot, his pupils way bigger than they should be. "You don't trust me?"

My heart skittered in my chest, my throat working to tell him that of course I trusted him, to proverbially pat him on the back until he let me go but instead I stood there, still as a statue, mute and brain dead.

"C'mon Nellie, I'm not so bad, am I?" His mouth relaxed slightly, his lips curving into a smile that had an edge to it that made something like fear slither up my spine. "At least I'm not crazy, right?" he whispered, bringing his face so close to mine that our noses bumped. "What about you, Nell? How's the old sanity these days?"

"W-what?" I stuttered, wedging my arms between the two of us so that my hands were resting palm down on his chest, shoving ineffectually.

His smile widened and his grip on me tightened. "Don't be shy. Paige tells me everything, Nellie. Everything."

My insides went completely still, my heart stopped beating inside my chest and I stopped trying to get away as I stared up at him with wide eyes. "Let me go," I croaked after a long beat of silence, my heart rate resuming at a much faster pace.

"Don't like it that I know your secrets, Nell?" Slowly, he raised one of his hands, brushing a strand of my long, light brown hair off my forehead, his fingers lingering on my skin longer than necessary. "For a crazy chick, you sure are uptight."

Crazy.

I shook my head, gasping in a sharp breath and then another, the sky feeling like it was falling in on me. "Let me go," I said, my voice barely a whisper.

Suddenly, he tilted his head back and gave a long, deep chuckle before releasing me. "Whatever you want." He turned his back on me, leaving me on the lawn in front of a house overflowing with teenagers doing all kinds of illegal things, the ground shaking from the loud music.

I could hear sirens in the distance and I knew it wouldn't be long before this party was busted.

My hands clenched into fists at my sides, my eyes following Brian until he disappeared into the house, his strides a bit unsteady, his shoulders a bit too stiff, like no matter how much he drank, he never quite got to that languid state, like he could never really relax.

I knew how that felt.

She told him.

I winced, turning my back on the house, raising a hand to place it on my chest, right over the deep ache that had settled there at his words.

What had I been thinking, coming here? Paige had been drinking more lately, even during the week and judging by the way she acted sometimes, she was doing more than just drinking. My footsteps halted and I looked over my shoulder back at the house, worried about her, pissed that I couldn't talk to her anymore, not like I used to.

I was starting to think it would never be the same between us, that I'd lost her.

Letting out a long, slow breath, I faced forward again, knowing going back in there would be pointless.

"I can fix this," I muttered, walking with my head down towards my beat up old car, the car I'd purchased with every penny I could scrape together from working at The Bean on the weekends and a couple nights a week.

Pressure built in my temples once again, my brain working hard to figure out a way to make things right between us, to get her to look at me like her sister again.

By the time I made it to my car, I had no solution.

In fact, I had another problem.

My car was boxed in. One car in front, one car behind each leaving about an inch of space between their bumpers and mine.

I let out a short laugh before throwing my head back and staring at the stars, automatically picking out the constellations I knew. Paige and I used to sneak out into the back yard and lie under the stars. I'd gone to the library, had studied for hours so I could point the constellations out to her.

Now it was all over. Now she saw me the same way everyone else did.

I closed my eyes and let out a short puff of air before leaning forward and resting my hands on the roof of my car, leaning my head in until it was against the cold metal, allowing some of the pressure in my brain to ease.

Slowly, piece by piece, I pulled myself together, straightening my spine and dragging my hands away from my car, my chin lifting to look over at the car parked mere inches in front of mine. With an angry twist of my lips, I edged towards it, my gaze drifting over the SUV, obviously a soccer mom car that little Timmy or whatever borrowed for the night.

Teeth gritted, I raised a foot and gently placed my sneaker on the front bumper before leaning my weight into it, rocking the vehicle but unfortunately, it didn't miraculously move far enough for me to drive the hell away from there.

"What the hell are you doing to my car?"

At the sound of the angry male voice way too close behind me, my foot slid off the bumper, throwing me off balance enough to knock me forward until I was on my knees in front of the damn SUV from hell.

"Shit," I muttered, lifting my hands to inspect the pebbles now embedded into my skin. "What's your problem?" I grumbled, craning my neck to glare at the guy lurking behind me, forgetting for a moment that I wasn't the kind of girl who swore, grumbled, or glared at strangers.

His face was in shadow so I couldn't really make out his features. He was definitely tall though and I didn't think it had anything to do with the fact that I was kneeling at his feet. His broad shoulders eclipsed the moon from this angle and I had a fleeting thought that I probably should apologize for kinda sorta kicking his car.

I opened my mouth to do just that when he said, "You're the one kicking my car, Cupcake. How am I the one with the problem?"

Cupcake? Did he just call me Cupcake?

"Hey," he said after a moment, leaning forward so that his face was almost level with mine, the night keeping his features in shadow, "why are you still on your knees, Cupcake?"

My teeth ground together and I glared at him as I stood up, anger making my hands clench into fists. "Look, sugarplum," I hissed, raising a hand to jamb my index finger into his chest, a part of my brain shocked at what I was doing. The other part, the part in control, didn't care. "You're the one parked two inches in front of my car. How am I supposed to get out of here?"

He shrugged. "Stay and party."

He lifted the bottle of clear liquid in his hands and took a deep swig from it, his hair falling over his forehead only to be brushed aside by an impatient hand.

I frowned, my gaze shifting to the house behind him, the music somehow even louder than it had been moments before. "I wasn't invited," I said stiffly, rubbing my palms on the thighs of my jeans. "Listen, just move your car, okay?"

"I can't."

"What? Why not?"

He gave a casual shrug of his shoulders and despite the dark, I could see the way his lips curled into a crooked grin. "I'm drunk, Cupcake. It wouldn't be very responsible of me to get in my car and drive."

The sound of sirens became even louder and I knew I didn't have long before they got here. "I'll do it," I said hastily, my voice holding an edge of panic that I hated as I held my hand out for his keys.

He gave a low chuckle, shaking his head as he stared down at me. "You're kidding, right? You expect me to let you drive my car?"

"Moving it forward a foot is hardly driving it," I said, casting a quick glance down the street, expected to see flashing lights at any moment. "C'mon, please," I whispered, ready to beg.

"Nope," he said, shifting so that he was leaning against my car, his face lit by the streetlamp. I blinked up at him, realizing that he looked familiar. Did he go to my school?

"Oh god," I muttered, my eyes widening when I spotted the flashing blue and red lights down the street, headed this way. "Oh my god, I'm going to get arrested." I couldn't get arrested. If that went on my record then I'd be finished. No school would admit me after that then I'd have to stay with my parents, I'd have to watch their eyes turn dark as I told them why I couldn't go to school, why I'd ruined my future.

The annoying asshole leaning against my car gave another chuckle and carelessly tossed the bottle of liquid onto the lawn far enough away that no one would suspect it was his. "You're not going to get arrested, Nell. You're not even doing anything illegal."

"This party is illegal and I'm here. I could easily get..." I trailed off, something clicking in my brain. "Did you just call me Nell?" I asked, craning my neck to get a better look at him, half his face in shadow still but the other half was definitely familiar. Something like unease settled in the pit of my stomach as a memory tried to breach the surface of my foggy brain but couldn't get past my panic. "Do I know you?"

He tilted his head to the side, staring down at me in silence for a moment before giving a slow shrug, looking completely relaxed even though the cop cars were just a few feet away, their sirens wailing, the lights flashing.

"What the hell is that supposed to mean?" I snapped, panic climbing up my throat as the cop cars stopped just up the street and officers started stepping out of the sedans. "Just give me the keys!" I half shouted, my hand reaching up and giving his shoulder a shove.

Wait, what? Had I just...pushed him?

I yanked my hand back down to the side, trying to get my breathing under control, my brain going nuts as cops started streaming over the sidewalk, heading for the house.

"Did you just push me, Cupcake?" he asked, leaning in closer to me, his voice lower than it had been before.

"No," I said, wincing as he raised a dark eyebrow. "Okay, yes. I'm sorry. Now please, let me move your car."

"I can't——"

"You can!" I shouted, my hands twitching with the need to push him again. What the hell was going on with me? I never lost my tempter. Never.

"No, Cupcake, I really can't. You see, this car——"

"Oh my god, let's get the fuck out of here," the high pitched and excited voice of a girl I didn't recognize said as she stepped up to the SUV, digging in her purse for something.

I blinked at her and her two friends who were obviously very drunk, each of the girls leaning their weight against the SUV.

Did they have the wrong car?

The girl finally found what she was looking for in her purse and held up a set of keys triumphantly before hitting the power lock button.

The telltale sound of doors unlocking reached my ears and seconds later, all three girls were in the SUV and driving away.

Slowly, anger simmering in my blood, I turned towards the guy still leaning casually against my car. "That SUV wasn't yours."

"Not technically."

"Then why," I asked, my voice low and maybe a little bit...menacing? Since when was I menacing? "did you tell me it was yours?"

"Look Cupcake, I was just kidding around."

"Don't," I snapped, "call me Cupcake. Now get the hell away from my car."

"I'm pretty comfortable here," he muttered, leaning his head back, settling more fully against my car.

"Oh my god," I muttered, my anger tipping into rage, every emotion that had been simmering inside of me shifting until my vision went red and I was suddenly angrier than I'd ever been. I stepped in front of him and without thinking it through, placed my hands on his chest, grabbing the lapels of his leather jacket. "Whatever your issue is, I don't care. I just want you to get off my fucking car you lowlife piece of scum!" My voice was shaking with fury and my fists kept tightening on the soft leather beneath my fingers.

His body stiffened as he straightened from the car only to lean forward, bringing his face closer to mine. Close enough that I could make out all his features clearly for the first time.

Scratch that, it wasn't the first time I'd seen him clearly.

That memory that had been nagging at me earlier, the one that just couldn't seem to surface? Yeah, now I remembered.

Grayson West. His name was Grayson West and he went to the same school as me. I'd seen him around, wearing his leather jacket, riding his motorcycle and one memorable time, I saw him beating the shit out of another guy behind the school.

And now I was antagonizing him.

My fingers went slack as everything inside of me went cold, my anger dying a quick death as his face came closer to mine and I realized that his eyes were such a dark shade of brown that they almost looked black. His lips had thinned into a flat line and there was a muscle in his strong jaw that was ticking ominously.

"Do you really think you should talk to me like that, Cupcake?"

Despite the low pitch to his voice and the menace in his face, a fresh bolt of anger still made its way through me at the stupid nickname.

"I——"

"Is there a problem here?" an officer cut me off, his flashlight shining right into my eyes, making me wince and look away.

"No problem, officer," Grayson said immediately, straightening his spine and shifting a step away from me, his lips stretching into what probably seemed like an unassuming, even bland smile but with the light shining on him, I could see the edge to his expression, the way his lips tightened at the corners, the way that muscle in his jaw continued to tick. Yeah, he was pissed off.

At me.

"My friend was just heading home," he said, cutting a glance over to me and the look in his eyes sent chills down my spine. How had I not realized it before? This guy was dangerous and I'd been aggravating him from the moment we'd set eyes on each other.

I swallowed hard, giving the officer a quick nod before stepping up to my car, pulling the door open and climbing in, holding my breath as my shoulder brushed against Grayson's. "See you around, Cupcake," he whispered as I brushed by him.

When the door was closed behind me, I took my first full breath since the streetlight had fully illuminated his face and I'd seen my life flash before my eyes.

When something tapped on my window, I jumped practically out of my seat, my heart rate skyrocketing dangerously but it was just the cop gesturing for me to roll down my window. "Have you been drinking?" he asked, once my window was down.

"No," I replied easily, relieved that it wasn't Grayson tapping his brass knuckles against my window or something.

"You sure?"

"Yeah," I said, nodding.

He shone his flashlight in my face, his gaze taking in my features, settling on my eyes as he leaned in closer and inhaled, smelling for alcohol before shifting back and saying, "Okay. Drive safely."

"Thanks," I muttered, turning my car on, listening as the engine made an odd, sputtering sound before turning over, allowing me to put it into gear and drive off.

My back was ramrod straight as I drove down the police lined street, my eyes wide, my breathing shallow and laboured.

...lowlife piece of scum.

"Holy shit," I whispered, taking a corner at a crawl. "I'm going to die, aren't I?" I asked the road in front of me, seeing an image of Grayson's fist slamming into that guy's face. I hadn't known the guy or Grayson, really. Of course, most people knew Grayson by reputation. He was the kind of guy you steered clear of, the kind of guy women crossed the street to avoid if they happened to see him walking towards them at night.

He was also the kind of guy that probably wouldn't let an insult go without some kind of retribution.

So yeah, I was probably dead meat.

"Awesome," I muttered, my foot inching down on the gas pedal a little more making the engine groan in protest, picturing the guy who'd been on the receiving end of Grayson's wrath, seeing the blood that had poured from his split lip, remembering the gash through his eyebrow.

"Awesome," I repeated, more quietly this time, my stomach turning at the thought of my almost certain ass kicking.

Shaking my head to clear the image, my mind flipped back over the events of the night, seeing my sister's face turn from drunkenly happy to darkly angry when she'd spotted me at the party, watching as she'd marched towards me, pure hate in her eyes, a look I'd seen before enough times to recognize.

Just not usually from her.

I shook my head, cutting of that train of thought, recognizing it as useless, feeling the way it made that ever present thing inside of my chest tighten and coil, cutting of my breath.

"It's okay," I whispered to myself, forcing my spine to relax, letting my fingers loosen their grip on the steering wheel enough so that my knuckles didn't ache. "I've got this." By the time I'd made it home, my body had relaxed, that tight coil inside of me had loosened enough that I could at least breathe normally and the pressure in my head wasn't so bad anymore.

I sighed, suddenly feeling exhausted as I pulled the handle and pressed my shoulder into the door to give it a hard shove, wincing at the horrible metallic scraping noise it made as it slowly opened.

Note to self, apply some oil to the hinges.

It took three tries to get the door shut and by the time I did, my eyelids were drooping. I stumbled toward my house, my eyes on the ground in front of me, not needing to look up to find my way to the front door.

The walkway was lit by those cute little lights that every house on this street had, the interlocking stones that made up our driveway were impeccably placed by only the best contractors. The house itself was beautiful. Large and designed to make people who couldn't afford it, want it. The inside was decorated by a professional, the paint on each wall hand picked by my mother, Eleanor, who had an eye for beauty and had built a business from the ground up based on that eye. My father, Dean, was a businessman. A good one. He made a reputation of picking up failing businesses and reshaping them until they were incredibly successful. Everywhere he went people would shake his hand and he'd flash them his wide smile, his light grey eyes flashing with charm as he wove his spell over them. He could talk his way out of anything, his good looks and charisma made people want to be near him, to gain his approval.

Together with my mother, who was still a stunning beauty at the age of forty five, they were the power couple of the neighbourhood. They were perfect.

Maybe that's why they hated me.

I didn't quite fit in with this beautiful family. My long, brown hair was a bit on the mousy side with a few darker streaks through it and none of the natural highlights that my sister had inherited from my mother. My eyes were a shade darker than my father's making them far less remarkable, my smile a touch too hesitant, lacking that easy charm that he wielded like a weapon.

My features didn't match my mother's in beauty, not even close. She and Paige shared the same sharp cheekbones and narrow facial structure, short, straight noses, and wide blue eyes. Paige's eyes had those grey flecks in them though, practically the only feature we shared.

My cheekbones were wider and not as sharp. My face rounder, more heart-shaped and my mouth wider, my lower lip a bit too pouty. My nose had a slight bump at the bridge and turned up a bit at the end. My skin was a shade darker than theirs too, no matter how little sun I got, I always looked like I had a bit of a tan.

Everyone knew I was the odd man out in this group and no matter how hard I worked to make it different, nothing ever changed.

I eased the front door open slowly, careful not to make any noise as I walked in a shut the door behind me.

I frowned as a familiar sensation stole over me. Unease.

I wasn't surprised when I felt that tightness in my chest, the same tightness I'd been feeling since I was six years old, ever since I'd nearly lost my mother at a shopping mall. It was odd how such a beautiful house filled with rich carpets and warm colours could make me feel so uncomfortable but every time I set foot inside, I felt like the air was just a bit too thick, like my lungs didn't know how to digest the oxygen they were breathing in.

Welcome home, I thought wryly, the term bringing a twisted smile to my lips.

I walked through the halls silently, making my way up the stairs and into my room where I let out a long, slow breath, allowing my body to relax, trying to ignore the white walls around me, the plain, white bedspread and the white curtains that rounded off the look. My room was always impeccably clean, nothing was ever out of place but I hated it. I hated every single pristine white inch of it.

I flicked on the light and moved to my bed, straightening out a tiny wrinkle in the white duvet. I changed quickly, exhaustion beating down on me, making my footsteps clumsy as I got ready for bed.

When I finally slid between the sheets, I sighed, ready to conk out, to forget everything that had happened that night and lose myself in a dreamless oblivion.

God, I was tired.

The whole weekend had been a bust. Every time I'd shut my eyes, I'd see either Grayson's dark eyes glaring at me or Paige's pretty blue eyes as they flashed in anger. I kept waking up, feeling like hands were wrapped around my throat, choking the air out of me while someone heavy sat on my chest, forcing what oxygen I did have out of my lungs.

Monday had come way too soon.

One more class, I encouraged myself, walking into Chemistry and taking my usual seat.

"Hey Nell," Craig Jenson said as he sank into the seat beside me, flashing me his usual charming grin. Craig was on the football team and was Brian's best friend. He'd stuck by him through the injury and had been looking out for him since he'd started his downward spiral.

Unfortunately, nothing seemed to be working.

Craig and I had formed an unlikely friendship when we realized that we were both trying to save someone who didn't want to be saved.

"Hey," I said, giving Craig a smile.

"I heard about the party," he said quietly, his lips turning down in a frown as his warm brown eyes scanned my features. "You okay?"

I shrugged, my lips tilting up in a half smile. "I'm fine. Nothing out of the ordinary." I paused for a second, noticing the tightness of his expression and the way he clenched his pencil so hard that it looked like it was about to snap. "Did you talk to Brian this weekend?"

His frown deepened as he nodded, running a hand through his light brown hair. "I think he's on something, Nell." I thought so too. "I just...I don't know what else to do."

"Craig," I said, resting my hand on his forearm, feeling kind of out of place offering him comfort but it would've been weird not to. "You know it's not up to you, right? That you can't blame yourself for something that's out of your control."

His eyes flashed over to me and the deep sadness in them had me catching my breath for a second. "Yeah," he said after a moment, pulling his arm away from my hand and straightening in his seat just as one of his buddies came over to our table and started talking to him.

Then the Craig from moments before was gone, replaced by Craig the jock, the guy who got along with everyone and hung out with the football team, the guy who didn't care about much of anything besides sports and girls.

This was our pattern. We had these brief flashes where we understood each other, where he didn't look at me like I was just another nerd he passed in the hallways and then, as soon as someone else was looking, we shifted back to our respective social circles.

I ignored the girls who leaned against my desk, each struggling to get closer to Craig as I straightened the notebook in front of me, lining up my pencil and my back up pencil perfectly so that their tops were parallel to my three pens, my eraser at the top of the desk, perpendicular to the writing utensils.

I looked over my homework and frowned, wondering if I'd managed to get everything right. It wasn't hard but thanks to my lack of sleep and full work schedule this weekend, I'd been unfocused.

I hated being unfocused.

Something prickled at the back of my neck and I frowned, raising my head to take a look around the class, feeling like someone was watching——

My heart stopped when my gaze connected with Grayson's, his dark eyes boring a hole into me, making me want to squirm in my seat.

My mouth dropped open when his lips stretched into a smile that was less than friendly as he leaned back in his chair, crossing his arms over his chest.

"Okay, class," Mr. Wright said, clapping his hands together as he stepped up to the chalkboard and wrote the title of the lesson down.

I yanked my gaze away from Grayson's, knocking my pencils out of order when I jerked forward.

What the hell was he doing there?

I waited for Mr. Wright to ask him why he was in his class and to subsequently kick him out but nothing happened.

He even looked right at him and didn't even bat an eye.

As Mr. Wright lectured, I couldn't pay attention, my mind focused on the tingles I could feel at the back of my neck, hoping that my exhaustion was making me see things and that Grayson hadn't really been there, sitting at the back of the class like he owned it.

"Nell," Mr. Wright said, his eyes landing on me as he pointing at the question on the board. "Care to answer this one?"

"Sure," I mumbled, my breath catching in my throat as I looked over the problem, trying to mentally catch up on what he'd been talking about.

Oh god, did I know the answer? Some of it looked familiar, had this been one of the homework questions?

I stepped up to the board and took the chalk Mr. Wright offered me, wondering why it felt so heavy, hating the feeling of everyone's gaze on me but most especially hating the feeling of Grayson's eyes. Why the hell could I feel his eyes boring into me?

I gave myself a mental shake, focusing on the question. Okay, I could do this. It was easy, just a simple compound and its formula. I began writing, my hand shaking a bit at first but as I made my way through the problem, my unease lifted, some of the tension in my shoulders draining away. Yeah, this was one of the homework problems I had worked on so of course I'd be——

"Wrong."

I blinked, everything inside of me going still at the low, deep voice from the back of the room.

"Let her finish, Mr. West."

"Sure, but she's wrong."

I was frozen where I stood, the chalk resting on the board, my breath coming in fast, shallow pants as my insides squeezed together painfully.

"Mr. West, take a seat!" Mr. Wright said sternly, his double chin wiggling in indignation.

"I'm just trying to help," Grayson said, his voice now way closer, so close that I could feel his breath on my cheek just before his hand covered mine, prying the chalk out of my lifeless fingers. "I got this one, Cupcake," he whispered, his low voice sending chills down my spine.

Oh shit, I knew I shouldn't have pushed him. I was always so in control, how could I have lost my temper with him of all people? Did I have a death wish?

"Cupcake?"

My head swung to the side, my eyes widening when I realized how close he was, his nose almost touching mine, so close that I could see the dark lashes framing his even darker eyes. Was that a scar through his eyebrow?

"Move."

I blinked and took a hasty step back before shuffling to my seat, my heart pounding furiously in my chest as Grayson solved the problem on the board.

"Correct," Mr. Wright said, a wry smile on his round face. "You must have been doing your homework, Mr. West, considering your attendance record."

Grayson just shrugged, handing the chalk back to Mr. Wright before turning towards the class. He sent a smug smile in my direction before passing by me, his hand casually reaching out and knocking my eraser onto the floor.

For the next forty-five minutes I forced myself to stay upright, to keep my hands on the desk and not pick up that eraser.

It didn't make sense and the longer I sat there, conscious of it beneath the desk, the tighter the coil in my chest got but if I did it, if I bent over and picked it up, I'd lose.

I had no idea what it was that I'd lose but the idea wrapped itself around my mind and wouldn't let go.

He couldn't win.

By the time class was over, my knuckles ached from having clenched my hands into fists for so long and there were deep, half moon marks in my skin from my fingernails but I'd done it. I'd gotten through the whole class without picking up that eraser. "See you tomorrow," Mr. Wright said freeing everyone for the day and with a long sigh, I leaned down to pick up my eraser.

It wasn't there. I scanned the area surrounding my desk but it was gone.

Frowning, I straightened and gathered my books, keeping my eyes on the floor for my eraser as I stood and walked towards the exit.

I saw his black boots a split second before I would've run into him, stopping myself barely an inch in front of his chest.

"Looking for this, Cupcake?" Grayson asked, holding my eraser so close to my face that my eyes crossed.

"Yes," I snapped, reaching up to grab it but he yanked it away and put it in his pocket.

"Mine now," he said, smiling smugly down at me. I blinked up at him, the slope of his nose grabbing my attention for a second. His nose was straight and long, almost...proud looking. But why was it so straight? Considering his tendency to get into fights, shouldn't it have been broken a time or two? Shouldn't it be kind of crooked?

Unless he never got hit.

I swallowed past the nervous lump in my throat and took a step back from him, needing some distance between the two of us. "W-why would you want my eraser?" I asked, my voice quivering just slightly.

He tilted his head to the side, his smile gone as his eyes darkened and his jaw hardened. "Because I'm a lowlife piece of scum, I guess."

I took another step back as a cold chill swept through me. "Look, about that..."

He quirked an eyebrow. "What? You didn't mean it?"

I opened my mouth to tell him that no, I didn't mean it, that I was sorry for saying it but for some reason, nothing happened. My throat wasn't working, my voice locked somewhere inside of me and I watched helplessly as his eyes darkened even further until they were two black pools of fury.

I took another step back.

"So I take it you did mean it," he said, his voice somehow even lower, menacing, as he took a step closer to me.

I shook my head, retreating another step.

"God, chicks like you piss me off. You think you're better than me because you live on the rich side of town?" I shook my head again, retreating until my back hit the wall, belatedly realizing that we were the only two people left in the classroom. "Do you think you're smarter than me because you can line up your pencils real nice and you've got a perfect attendance record?" He advanced until he was right in front of me, the toes of his boots brushing against the toes of my sneakers. "You're not the one who solved the problem, are you, Cupcake?"

"Leave me alone," I croaked, my pulse racing and my legs shaking from fear. Why hadn't I just apologized? Why didn't I just tell him I was sorry and be done with it? Now I was going to get my ass kicked and it was all my fault.

"Are you afraid of me, Cupcake?" he asked, leaning in even closer, resting his hand just behind my head, using the wall to hold his weight.

I opened my mouth to tell him that yes, I was scared of him, the beg him to leave me alone. I sucked in a breath and said, "Fuck you."

Silence.

I stopped breathing as my own words registered, my heart going still in my chest when his eyes narrowed and his whole face darkened with anger.

After a long beat of silence, he said, "Do you really want to fuck with me, Nell?"

No!

I tried to push the word out but when I opened my mouth, I said, "Keep the eraser, Grayson," and ducked under his arm, hoofing it to the door.

I almost made it too until he grabbed my wrist, stopping me.

And just like that, something inside of me snapped.

"Let me go," I said, my voice lower than normal, and strangely steady.

"You——"

"I said," I snapped, yanking on my arm until he released, "let go!" I wrapped both my arms around my books and glared at him, suddenly so mad that I couldn't think straight. "You hate chicks like me?" I hissed, advancing towards him even as all my defense mechanisms screamed for me to run away. "You hate me because I live on the rich side of town? Well I hate guys like you who think they're all that just because they're a bit taller and stronger than someone. So yeah, fuck you Grayson West. You're not so scary, you know that?" I tilted my head back and laughed, feeling just as crazy as everyone thought I was. "And you know what?" I screeched, advancing once more until we were toe to toe, raising my hand and pushing him on the shoulder. "My name is not Cupcake!"

"God, you're nuts," he snarled, bringing his face closer to mine, not budging an inch even when I pushed him again. "You look all calm on the outside until someone flips the switch and BAM, you go crazy!"

"Don't call me crazy!" I shouted like a lunatic.

"Just calling 'em as I see 'em, baby."

I made a frustrated sound, rolling my eyes at him. "My name isn't baby either."

"You're just as uptight as you look, baby."

"I'm only uptight when jerks are lying to my face about the car that's blocking me in."

"I was just messing around. Can't you take a joke?"

"I had a bad night and you were being a total asshole to me, so no, I can't take a joke!"

"Loosen up, Cupcake, it wasn't——"

"I can't!" I screamed, dropping my books on the floor to shove him as hard as I could, hard enough that he actually had to take a step back to keep his balance. We stayed like that for a second, me with my hands on his chest, his arms raised instinctively, his long fingers circling my wrists as he stared at me like I was some strange species of animal he'd never seen before. I let out a long breath, my shoulders sagging and all the fight going out of me as I pulled my hands from his. "I can't," I repeated, more calmly this time, my face burning as I realized I'd just totally lost my mind in front of possibly the most dangerous guy in school.

My breathing was ragged as I knelt down and collected my books, abandoning a pencil that had slid too far from me. Without meeting his gaze, I turned my back and left, mortification making my skin crawl as I walked the hallways in a daze.

Had I lost my mind? Was it not enough that I'd risked life and limb on Friday, did I have to cement my death wish by having a shouting match with Grayson today, too?

I stopped in front of my locker, taking a moment to clear my mind of Grayson, deciding that if he wanted to finish me off, I probably wouldn't be able to stop him.

Should I feel better now?

I sighed and reached inside of my locker, packing up my bag with the books I'd need that night. It was Monday and I already had a ton of homework. I couldn't let things pile up, not now, not when I was so close. We'd gotten our report cards that day and judging by my marks, I'd get into any college I wanted.

I frowned as I shut my locker a little harder than necessary, the thought of college making my breath whoosh out of my lungs. College would be harder, more studying, more work, I already felt like I was being buried. I had no social life, no friends...would it always be like this?

My fingers clutched the straps of my bag tightly, the world around me spinning out of control, my life flashing before my eyes and from the glimpses I got it looked...empty, unlived.

Is that what I wanted?

I shook my head and straightened my shoulders, telling myself I was being ridiculous. Of course I wanted to go to college, to work hard...to make my parents proud.

I'd already put in so much work, I'd see it through.

I just had to stay away from people like Grayson West. Next time I saw him, I wouldn't even say anything. I'd just look right through him and forget about him.

The thought made me feel better and my shoulders relaxed as I exited the school, taking the steps slowly, not in a rush to get home and start on my homework.

I froze when I saw a familiar motorcycle at the bottom of the steps. Grayson's black eyes locked on mine as he pulled down the visor on his helmet and gave me a salute.

I didn't react. I stood still and watched as he started his bike and revved the engine, his head turned towards me, the weight of his gaze burning into me but I remained unfazed, my earlier lunacy forgotten as I waited for him to le——

"See you later, Cupcake!" he shouted above the roar of the motorcycle.

I gave him the finger.

So much for forgetting about him.

Chapter 2

I pushed my potato salad across my plate, my eyes locked on my report card sitting on the table next to me. I'd gotten all A's.

My gaze slid to the head of the table where my dad sat, his reading glasses perched at the edge of his nose, his attention focused on the paper in his hand, not even bothering to look as he forked food into his mouth.

I glanced over at my mother, noticing that she was reading a magazine, her back perfectly straight, her expression her usual mix of boredom and disdain that never failed to make me feel like I was somehow failing her.

Putting my fork down, I cleared my throat, trying to get their attention. Neither of them moved, their gazes remaining on their reading material.

I bit my lip, that ugly, coiled thing inside of me winding tighter as my fingers started to shake making my fork hard to grip. I set it down and placed my hands in my lap, curling my fingers inward until I was making fists when I cleared my throat again.

When they still didn't look I decided that the direct approach was necessary. "I got my report card today," I said, my voice flat, almost businesslike.

My father made a noncommittal sound while my mother didn't make any move as if she'd heard me.

Letting out a long, slow breath, I shifted my gaze to my hands in my lap, fidgeting slightly in my seat, wishing I could go outside because the air in the dining room just wasn't cutting it anymore. I reached up and tugged at the neck of my blouse, wanting to undo a button but just then my mother looked up, her eyes latching onto where my hand was before her gaze connected with mine, a knowing light in her eyes that made me stop breathing altogether and had my hand dropping back into my lap so fast that I practically punched my thigh.

Her lids lowered slightly, her blue eyes turning icy as they shifted over my face, probably noting how red I was turning on account of the lack of air in my lungs. Why did this always happen to me? Why did she make me feel like this?

Her lips thinned just before she shifted in her seat and opened her mouth to say something but before she got the chance, the front door opened and the sound of high heeled shoes on tile made her mouth snap shut. My father put down his paper and all three of us turned our heads towards the entrance to the dining room.

"Did I miss dinner?" Paige asked, popping her head around the corner, her smile wide and a little wobbly as she teetered towards us on heels that were way too high for her. Her cheeks were red and her hair was disheveled. Her shirt was on inside out and her eye makeup was running but she still looked beautiful.

She also looked drunk.

I winced when she stumbled and used a nearby wall to steady herself as she kicked off her shoes and leaned her head back to groan in ecstasy. "Much better," she mumbled, walking around the table towards Eleanor, planting a loud kiss on her mother's cheek before collapsing into the chair next to her. "This looks so good," she said, reaching out to the roast chicken slices in the centre of the table, filling her plate with mashed potatoes and covering everything with gravy.

"Paige, what do you think you're doing?" Eleanor snapped, pulling the fork from my sister's hand.

"Eating," she replied with an eye roll before reaching across the table for my fork.

"You've been drinking," Eleanor hissed, leaning closer to my sister, her icy gaze moving over Paige, pausing whenever something met with her disapproval.

"Yup," Paige said, flashing me a broad grin. "What of it?"

Eleanor's eyes lit with anger and she opened her mouth to speak but my father cut her off. "Let her be, Eleanor." His tone was mild, bored even as he continued to read the newspaper in front of him. "If she wants to act like an idiot then she can. Just as long as she gets it out of her system before tomorrow."

"Hm," Paige said, grinning around a mouthful of potatoes. "I'm not sure I can do that, Dad."

Dean's eyes snapped up from his paper, latching onto Paige's gaze in a way that made me squirm even though it wasn't me he was looking at. "Tomorrow is the Johnston's dinner party. You will be there and you will be sober, are you hearing me? This dinner is important to my business and if you do anything to mess it up, I will kick you out of this house without batting an eye."

Paige's jaw tightened but she nodded as my father shifted his attention away from her and that oppressive silence that seemed to hang over our heads whenever we were near each other threatened to suffocate me once more.

"May I be excused?" I mumbled, willing my voice to remain steady, to not give away how uncomfortable I felt around my family and how much it terrified me to think of the next night at the Johnston's. What if I couldn't hold it together? What if the air got too stuffy and people started asking me too many questions? What if I lost control?

My parents made noncommittal sounds and I pushed my chair away from the table making as little noise as possible. Just before I turned to leave, Paige caught my eye and for a brief moment, nothing had changed. That spark of understanding was right there in her blue eyes, that connection we'd always shared clear and strong once again.

Then her lip curled in disgust and she mouthed, "Fuck you."

I turned on my heel and left, my spine stiff and my report card clutched in my hand. Why had I even brought it there? I hadn't really expected them to care, I just thought——

Suddenly the piece of paper was ripped from my hands, tearing it nearly in two before I released my half and twisted to face my sister who was holding the scraps of my report card. The door to the dining room quietly slid shut behind us as I turned towards her, automatically reaching out to retrieve what was mine.

"All A's," Paige said, twisting her body to avoid my hand. "Impressive, Nell. I'm so sorry I ripped it. Now how are mom and dad going to stick it on the fridge?" she asked, holding the paper behind her as I made another grab for it.

"Just give it back Paige."

"Why? So you can show it to them again? So you can bask in their praise? You know they don't give a shit, Nell." I frowned, my gaze connecting with hers as I forgot about reaching for my paper, suddenly tired of this dumb game we were playing.

"You're acting like a kid, Paige. Sober up and give me my report card back."

She tilted her head to the side and her eyes lit with satisfaction as she stared at me for a long beat before shrugging. "Fine," she said, her lips tilting into a lopsided smile. "Have it." She held the ripped paper out to me and I took it, ignoring the way my fingers practically tingled with the need to smooth it out and to tape the ripped part.

"Thanks," I mumbled, turning my back on her to go to my room.

"No matter what your GPA is, you're still going to be the crazy one." My footsteps froze, her words, lined with cruelty, hitting me like a kick to the spine. "And no matter how drunk I get, they'll still pick me over you, Nell. Nothing you do now will impress them, not after what you put us all through."

"Paige——"

"What?" she snapped, cutting me off. "Are you going to tell me you're sorry? Maybe you'll try to tell me that I don't understand?"

"You don't," I said, turning to face her, my heart beating fast in my chest, my hand clutching my report card so hard that it crumpled into a ball.

Her lips tightened and her eyes narrowed, anger shining from every line of her face. "Then explain it to me."

I winced, taking an involuntary step back at the same time. I couldn't do this. I couldn't explain it all to her when I barely understood it myself. "Paige, I——"

"Forget it," she said, rolling her eyes as she moved past me, bumping her shoulder hard into mine as she went by, making me stumble. "Wouldn't want you to strain the fragile balance that's going on up there." She pointed at my temple, her lips stretching into a sneer before she turned her back on me, heading towards the stairs.

My stomach sank and my heart clenched as I watched her walk away from me. "It doesn't have to be like this, Paige," I said softly, my voice wavering slightly with emotion.

She paused on the stairs, her shoulders stiff as she turned her face towards me. Her eyes were hard, frozen as she looked me from head to toe, finally letting her gaze rest on mine as she said, "Yes, it does," before continuing up the stairs.

Come watch the stars with me, Nell.

I blinked the slight moisture from my eyes, telling myself to brush it off, that one day I would be able to fix this.

One day we could go back to being Nell and Paige without all the other shit hanging over us.

Oh god, I was going to be late.

The dinner party was starting in ten minutes and I was stuck at the school with a car that would not start.

"C'mon," I mumbled for the millionth time, turning the key in the ignition, praying to any god available to just make the damn thing start.

My heart was beating rapidly against my rib cage, my throat was getting that tight, itchy feeling that I hated and everything inside of me was wound so tight that it felt like something might snap.

"Shit!" I shouted, banging my hand against the steering wheel when once again, the engine failed to turn over. "This can't be happening."

With another curse, I gathered my purse and stepped out of my car, shivering as the wind whipped at my legs, exposed by the dress I was wearing. I'd changed at school, knowing I wouldn't have enough time to get home after editing the paper.

So there I stood in a deserted parking lot, wearing a beige dress and little else to fight off the chill that easily penetrated the material and sunk into my skin.

Panic was starting to make its way up my throat and I tried to force myself to take a few calming breaths. When that didn't seem to help, I reared back my foot and kicked the front tire which logically, shouldn't have helped but for some reason that panic threatening to choke me receded just enough for my brain to click back on.

A cab. I could call a cab.

Feeling like an idiot for not thinking of it sooner, I pulled my cell phone out of my purse and dialled the number with shaking fingers.

"City Taxi, how can I help you?" the operator asked.

"Hi," I said on a sigh, my heart rate starting to calm down. "Can I get a cab at——"

The honk of a horn cut me off and I looked up to see Craig, driving close to me, rolling down his window as he approached. "Hey Nell!" he said, cutting his engine as he smiled at me. "Need a lift?"

"Yes," I said on a sigh, relief making the clawing panic evaporate. I mumbled an apology to the woman on the other end of the line and climbed into the passenger seat of Craig's shiny blue truck.

"You really need a new car, Nell," he said as he pulled away from the school and out of the parking lot.

"Yeah, I know," I said sending him a grateful smile. "I really appreciate this, Craig."

"No problem," he said, sending me a brief grin in return. "Where to?"

I gave him directions to the Johnston's house and by the time we pulled up to the massive colonial, I was only five minutes late.

"Thanks Craig, I owe you big time," I said, opening the door and jumping out of the truck.

"Give me your answers to the chemistry homework for a week and we're even."

I chuckled lightly, feeling a little lighter all of a sudden, like sometimes things didn't have to be so hard, that sometimes things just worked out. "Deal," I replied, shutting the door and giving him a wave over my shoulder as I made my way to the house.

A man in a tux greeted me, offering to take the light jacket I had around my shoulders. I handed him the coat, ignoring the anxiety that was creeping its way into my stomach at the thought of facing the crowd of people inside. I focused on my breathing as the man guided me to the cocktail lounge where everyone was gathering before dinner. I thanked him, smoothing out my features as he opened the door and I slipped inside.

I scanned the men and women inside, my eyes flashing over their expensive looking outfits, mentally taking note of the familiar faces there. Almost everyone here was a prominent member of the community and they all did business with my father. Many of them had brought their children as well and that bubble of anxiety inside of me grew slightly. I went to school with a few of these people and I didn't exactly run in the same social circles as them. In fact, I didn't really run in any social circlewhich worked just fine for me.

When I finally spotted my parents at the far side of the room, some of my anxiety faded and I began moving towards them through the people, keeping a polite smile planted on my face.

My smile didn't falter when a girl who went to my school gave me a dismissive glance, her eyes taking in my plain dress in one swoop, the twist of her mouth telling me without words that she was unimpressed. I kept my smile in place even when my gaze locked on Celia Blaire, one of my mother's closest friends and her eyes narrowed as she looked at me, her distaste clear on her face.

No, my smile didn't falter until my gaze connected with my mother's and all the blood drained from her face.

She looked beautiful in a deep red dress that showed off her still shapely figure and despite her drastic loss of colour, she was still very striking. In a few quick strides, she was next to me, her fingers wrapped around my arm and she subtly guided me towards my father and sister who were staring at me as if I were a particularly hard to shake piece of dirt on their shoes.

"Mom, what———?"

"What the hell do you think you're doing here?" she hissed in my ear after glanced around her, making sure no one could hear her.

I frowned, something uncomfortable and cold settling in the pit of my stomach. "What do you mean?" I whispered back, running my hands nervously over the bodice of my dress, hoping to smooth out any perceived wrinkles. "Dad said yesterday that we had to be here."

She gave me an incredulous look as we both came to a stop in front of Dean and Paige. "He said Paige needed to be here, not you. Do you have any idea how embarrassing this is?" she snapped, her eyes spitting fire even as she kept a placid look on her face, smiling gently at me.

My gaze slid over to my sister who tipped her glass of juice at me, giving me a sarcastic grin before taking a sip.

My lungs were starting to lock up, my brain turning cold as I shook my head slightly, confused. "I-I thought he meant for both of us to be here. I——"

"Just get her out of here, Eleanor," my father said in a low voice, his tone made of pure ice as he turned to great a man I recognized as the mayor who was heading this way.

"Come with me," Eleanor said, her grip on my arm tightening as she led me towards a side door, away from the crowd.

Confusion swamped me as I mentally tried to go over last night at the dinner table, trying to remember exactly what my father had said and whether or not I had been included in the invitation.

Shouldn't I have been?

The whole family had been invited, hadn't they?

"Eleanor," Celia Blaire said, stepping into our path, her lips tipped up in a smug grin. "Leaving so soon?"

My mother gave the woman a polite smile, her face a mask of civility as she said, "I'm afraid Penelope isn't feeling well and has to leave."

Celia's eyes connected with mine as she smiled softly. "That's really too bad. I was hoping to have a chance to...catch up with you, Nell. It's been so long. In fact, I'm quite sure I haven't seen you since the beginning of last summer. It was as if you disappeared for a couple months."

My heart stopped as the other woman's eyes lit with satisfaction. My mouth dropped open but speaking was impossible. My brain had stopped working and that thing in my chest was coiled so tight that it hurt.

"Some other time," my mother said, sidestepping Celia, her hand tightening on my arm even further, probably leaving bruises.

I blinked when we were out of the lounge room, my eyes taking in the paintings on the walls, the bricks around the fireplace, the couches spaced strategically around the room. The lights seemed too bright in there, even the flicker of the fireplace hurt my eyes and for some reason, my ears were ringing like I'd been standing next to a loud speaker for too long.

"…do this to me? To your father? What were you thinking?"

I blinked, finally focusing on my mother, her eyes livid, her face no longer a mask of polite disinterest as she glared at me as if I was the lowest form of life.

"I thought I was invited," I said softly, my voice sounding weird, lifeless and muffled to my own ears.

She gave a short laugh, pacing back and forth in front of me. "You must be joking. Do you know how long it took me to quiet the rumours about you over the summer? Everyone had their own theories of where you went and it took months to get them to stop speculating. You know how important these contacts are to your father and to have them questioning the stability of his own child would be a disaster. They'd all but forgotten about you but now…" She shook her head. "After everything you put me through last summer…"

The coil inside of me wound tighter until I felt like I might keel over from the pain. "You're the one who sent me away, Mom," I whispered, even as I told myself to let it drop, that if I didn't leave now, everything I'd worked for would be ruined.

Her eyes lit with renewed anger as she glared at me. "You were out of control, Nell. I had no choice."

Liar!

My heart pounded hard in my chest as bile rose in my throat.

"Out of...control," I repeated, my voice barely above a whisper.

"Yes," she hissed.

I nodded and an odd sense of calm stole over me even as the coil inside of me wound ever tighter, suffocating me from inside out. Oxygen didn't seem to matter so much right now. My eyes locked on my mother's and I saw in them what I'd been seeing for most of my life, disdain, anger, and below that, a layer of indifference that tore at me. "Things are never going to change between us, are they?" I whispered, my words seeming to echo off the vaulted ceilings and reverberate around us.

Her eyes for one moment flashed with an emotion that was gone before I could place it and then they were shuttered, locked down tight, replaced by the cool glare I was all too familiar with.

She leaned in close to me, her eyes never once leaving mine as she said in a low voice, "Grow up, Nell," before spinning on her heel and leaving me, going back to the party that I was not invited to.

When the door slid shut behind her, something inside of me shifted...

Or maybe shifted wasn't the right way to describe it.

No, it was more like...snapped, something inside of me snapped and that coil that had been wound so tight moments before, disappeared.

I frowned, rubbing the spot on my chest that had been aching so hard moments ago but now simply felt numb. What was going on with me? My breathing wasn't ragged anymore but that ringing in my ears was still there. When I started to walk away, my footsteps sounded muffled and everything around me still seemed too bright.

I felt changed, irrevocably changed in a way I couldn't put my finger on at the moment.

Grow up, Nell.

Those words should sting, right? I'd been trying for as long as I could remember to change things between Eleanor and me and with those two words, she'd decimated everything I'd worked for.

No matter how hard I tried, nothing was going to change.

God, I was so fucking sick of trying.

I tried to make her happy, tried to make my dad just look at me and I kept trying to save Paige.

Who the hell was I to save anyone? I could barely talk to another human being without hyperventilating and here I was trying to save someone?

What a joke.

But if I stopped trying, if I no longer cared about the report cards or the test scores or the college application...or Paige...

If I stopped caring about what my parents thought about me and focused instead on what I wanted...

Then what?

I didn't even know what I wanted to do with my life. I just figured I'd get into a good college, that I'd prove to Dean and Eleanor that I wasn't crazy, that I wasn't an embarrassment and then...

I let out a short bark of laughter, shaking my head, thinking about all the times I'd imagined it.

Eleanor would smile and hug me, handing Dean a camera so he could take a picture of the two of us, mother and daughter and then Dean would give the camera to a passerby, claiming that he needed a picture of all of us, the whole family with his little graduate and I would look at that picture and see the pride in their expressions and what? My life would be all rose coloured with a chance of rainbows?

I really was delusional.

I shook my head, realizing suddenly that I'd been walking for a while now and had somehow made my way to a lower floor. I heard the sounds of a kitchen as people prepared a meal for the guests above and the smells made my mouth water. I'd forgotten to eat lunch, too focused on getting all my homework done so I could make it to the party on time.

Idiot.

Following the sounds, I made my way down a hallway, stepping to the side when the doors to the kitchen burst open and waiters began streaming through, their arms loaded with plates filled with food. I flattened myself against the wall, watching blankly as my heart beat slow and steadily in my chest, an odd, chilly sensation creeping over my skin as I wondered why I felt so calm.

My gaze shifted to the side and I saw a bottle of champagne sitting on a small table off to my left.

I should take that.

I looked away from it as soon as the thought occurred, dismissing it for a little piece of crazy that I definitely didn't need in my life. If I got caught stealing a bottle of champagne from the Johnston's dinner party...

The thought made my chest tighten in a familiar way. Just thinking about seeing my mother with her lips curled in disgust and my father shaking his head at me in that way he did made my breath come a little faster.

I took a step away from the bottle, most of the kitchen staff now in the hall, handing out plates of food. I took another step and froze, my gaze sliding up and down the corridor, seeing no one else to confront me, no one to see, no one to ever know.

Before I knew what I was doing, I had that bottle in my hand and I was walking with quick steps towards the exit, a wide smile on my face as my heart raced in my chest.

There, I thought, my grin stretching even wider as I kept the champagne close to my side, hiding it from anyone who I may pass, I did it.

I wound my way through the hallways, eventually making it to an exit, my grin never once fading as I held my prize close to me. I let out an involuntary shiver when I stepped outside, the cold air slicing easily through my dress, my arms bare to the wind.

With one last look over my shoulder, I started walking along the driveway, the tight coil in my chest getting a little looser with each step. What did I care what they thought of me? If someone looked out the window right now and saw me walking down the driveway with no jacket and a bottle of champagne in my hands, they'd just call me crazy and have a good laugh.

I was done arguing with them, done trying to prove myself to a bunch of people who'd prefer to step on me than serve me dinner.

"Fuck 'em," I mumbled, working on the foil around the cork in the champagne then moving on to the metal part holding it down. "Grow up, Nell," I hissed, sending an angry glare at the house behind me just before I stepped onto the sidewalk. "Fine," I snapped, popping the cork and watching it fly, putting my lips to the opening to stop the liquid from hitting the ground.

After a few solid gulps, I used the back of my hand to wipe my mouth, the simple movement giving me joy because if my mother ever saw me do that, she'd give me one of those looks of hers, the ones that meant she was disappointed or disgusted or embarrassed.

I got those looks a lot and up until this point, I'd let them cut right through me, I'd become her little puppet, hoping that one day she'd change her mind about me.

"Disgusting," I muttered, taking a large swig, satisfied with the way the bubbles felt on their way down my throat.

I was walking quickly, barely pausing between sips, my steps taking me as far from the Johnston's mansion as possible, anger boiling in the pit of my stomach as I thought of all the times I'd held my tongue, all the times I'd put my own feelings aside so I could please my parents, constantly waiting for them to…

To what?

Accept me? Look at me?

Love me?

I felt a slight pang in my chest at the thought before dismissing it, hating it even as it appeared in my mind. It shouldn't be like that. I shouldn't have to work so fucking hard just to get them to care.

I was done with it. After tonight, they made it abundantly clear that no amount of work was going to change the way they looked at me.

From here on out, I was going to do what I wanted, when I wanted to do it and forget about the consequences.

The thought made me smile and I went to take another swig, noticing the bottle was more than half gone.

I saluted the tree next to me, grinning so hard that my cheeks hurt, not caring about the cold anymore. In fact, I felt kind of warm, like the thought of doing what I wanted for once was making a nice glow heat me up from the inside out.

I laughed out loud, feeling a bit like the crazy person everyone accused me of being and not caring. Instead, I tried to figure out what I wanted to do now that I didn't have to worry about gaining their approval.

I blinked at a rusty street sign, my eyes having a hard time focusing enough to actually read it so I opened them up wider and took a look around me.

I was in a neighbourhood I'd never seen before. The houses here were smaller and a lot more run down than the houses in the area the Johnston's lived in. I frowned, trying to think back over my walk, mentally retracing my steps in order to figure out where the hell I was.

I couldn't.

I tilted my head back and laughed, flinging my hands out to the side not giving a shit how crazy I looked. What did it matter? Everyone already thought I was mentally unhinged, why not give them something real to base it on. "I'm lost!" I shouted, my voice echoing down the empty street.

With a chuckle, I continued forward, taking another swig from my champagne bottle.

Grayson's POV

There was something about being on a bike that just put me at ease.

I loved the way it hugged the curves, the way the machine and I moved in time to create a balance. I loved that I could feel the barely restrained power underneath me as the engine rumbled.

But more than that, I loved the way the wind brushed past me with no barriers. In a car I felt like a sardine in a can but on a bike…I was free.

Of course, there were downsides. Like tonight, when there was a chill in the air, the wind had the tendency to find every inch that wasn't covered well enough and blast you. I shivered as I rounded a corner, thankful for my leather jacket but wishing I had worn something under it besides a t-shirt.

I didn't take the long way to my house that night like I normally would, prolonging my ride after my shift. No, tonight I wanted to be home where it was warm as soon as possible.

I hit the gas a little harder, pushing past the speed limit, knowing that there wouldn't be any cops around at this time of night on a Wednesday.

I was about a block away from my house when I spotted her. She was walking in a zigzag pattern on the sidewalk, her legs and arms bare with only a thin looking dress for coverage. Was she nuts? She must've been freezing.

I slowed down as I got closer to her, wondering if she was from the neighbourhood.

When she turned slightly, I frowned as a hint of recognition crept into my consciousness even as I shook it off. No, no way…

It couldn't be…

I squinted harder, getting closer every second and even though it seemed impossible…

It was Nell.

Nell Watson, rich girl and all around privileged chick was walking down my street in the middle of the night.

I slowed to a stop right next to her and noticed the large, empty bottle in her hand.

Perfect. Little miss rich girl was also completely hammered judging by the way she was walking. What the hell? Couldn't she just get drunk at a party like a normal person? Did she really have to be walking down my street, loaded and freezing?

I should just leave her there. If the positions were reversed, she wouldn't even hesitate.

Only…

It was seriously getting chilly out and that dress…

She was going to freeze.

"Hey," I said, my voice gruff from irritation as I pulled up beside her, pushing back the visor on my helmet.

She jumped, hugging the bottle to her chest as she turned towards me, her big grey eyes wide as saucers as she focused on me.

"What the hell are you doing, Cupcake?"

She blinked and her skin went from being pink from the cold, to pasty white, all the colour draining away as she slowly looked down at the bottle in her hands. "I-I-I…" She shook her head and in one smooth motion, gripped the bottle in one hand and lobbed it into a nearby bush. "Nothing," she said, brushing her hands over her stomach and down her thighs, smoothing out her dress as she straightened her spine and tilted her nose up in my direction. "Just…walking," she said, motioning to the sidewalk in front of her, the movement causing her to wobble slightly. Suddenly her eyes narrowed and focused on me, her finger pointing accusingly at my chest. "And don't call me Cupcake."

I narrowed my eyes at her finger, feeling a muscle in my cheek twitch. Even when she was wasted, she was uptight. "You're on my side of town now, Cupcake. I'll call you whatever I want to."

She frowned, her head turning from one side to the other, taking in the low income houses that were constantly falling apart and in need of repair before looking back at me, her eyes wide and her face white once again. "Your side of town?" she repeated, her voice trembling slightly as she wrapped her arms around her torso.

My lip curled and anger flared in my chest at the move. That's right, Cupcake, be afraid. "Look, why don't you just call your Daddy or driver or whatever and get a ride home. You're going to freeze out here."

She flinched slightly and took a step back from me, shaking her head as she tripped over a crack in the sidewalk and had to flare her arms to keep her balance. "I'll walk," she muttered, taking a step in the wrong direction, tripping slightly again before continuing.

I let out a long breath, tilting my head back to glare at the sky for a moment before I got off my bike and pulled my helmet off, planting it on the seat before striding after the girl who was forcibly implanting herself on my bad side. "Listen," I said, reaching out and wrapping my fingers around her arm. For a second I paused, surprised by how soft her skin was despite the goosebumps I could feel on her flesh.

"Let me go, jerk," she hissed, yanking her arm out of my grip without glancing back at me.

All thoughts of soft skin flew from my mind as I narrowed my eyes and took two angry steps after her, grabbing her arm once again and turning her toward me. "You're going the wrong way, Cupcake," I snarled right in her face, putting on my best 'bad guy' glare.

She blinked up at me, a few wrinkles appearing between her brows before she glanced behind me and said, "Oh." Then she calmly removed her arm from my grip and stepped around me, now heading in the right direction, her steps still wobbly but filled with new determination.

I ground my teeth together, exhaustion and anger eating at me as I watched her walk in that ridiculous dress, telling myself to just let her go, that she wasn't worth the trouble, that it would serve her right if she got frost bite or if someone tried to mug her.

Apparently I wasn't listening because five seconds later, I was right beside her, her shoulders gripped in my hands as I forced her to look at me, to see reason. "You can't walk all the way home, all right? If you're not going to call anyone, I'll take you home," I said through gritted teeth, motioning towards my bike parked next to the sidewalk.

She let out a stifled laugh, her manicured fingers moving to cover the smirk on her face at the thought of me giving her a ride. That muscle in my jaw started to twitch a little faster.

"Not a chance," she said, her voice trembling with laughter.

Suddenly, I didn't give a shit if she had an army of concerned parents to call for a ride, no one but me was taking her home and she was going to sit on my bike even if it killed me to get her there.

"Want to bet, Cupcake?" I said, my voice low and deceptively calm as I tightened my hold on her.

Her eyes met mine squarely, something in her gaze solidifying as she straightened her spine and glared at me. "What's the point in making a bet with you? There's nothing you have that I would ever want," she snapped.

Fresh anger swirled through my veins, making my lip curl back from my teeth, my fingers tightening on her shoulders before I let her go and gave a strained laugh. "That's right. I don't know what I was thinking. You of all people would never get on a motorcycle with someone like me. Imagine what would happen if someone saw us? What would people say? You're so concerned with how everyone sees you that you'd probably have a total meltdown if anyone knew you even spoke to me, never mind got onto the back of my bike. Pristine little Nell Watson's reputation tarnished from one ride on a motorcycle with the wrong guy. Your life would be over."

I blinked when her fist lashed out, catching me square in the chest. It didn't hurt but I couldn't help but reach up and place a hand right over the spot she'd hit me, too shocked to do much more than stare at her as she swung her arm back to repeat the move. "If you think you have any influence over my life, you're mistaken, Grayson."

"So if it's not the threat to your reputation that's holding you back then what is it, Nell?" I spat out, invading her space and bringing my face close to hers, trying to make her back up but she kept her ground, her gaze never once faltering. "Maybe you're just scared, is that it?"

Her eyes narrowed but she said nothing.

"That's it, isn't it? Are you afraid of the bike?" I could hear her teeth grinding together. "No?" I leaned in closer to her, my lips tilting up into a smug grin as I whispered in her ear, "Then is it me you're scared of, Cupcake?"

Her hands planted on my chest and gave a firm shove and I stepped back, mostly because I was surprised that she had the guts to push me at all. Her cheeks were red and her eyes were burning as she glared up at me, her chest rising and falling rapidly but still she didn't say anything. Then she was turning on her heel and before I could even think to chase after her, she was swinging her leg over my bike, adjusting her skirt so that she was covered to her knees before picking up my helmet and shoving it onto her head. Then she just sat there, her arms crossed over her chest, waiting.

I stared at her for a long beat, disbelief warring with respect in my head.

"Well?" she snapped, turning her head to glare at me, the helmet looking way too big on her, her long brown hair swirling over her shoulders in a mass of tangles making me think of all the times I'd seen her, unable to come up with one instance where every part of her appearance wasn't perfectly in control. "Are you going to drive me home or what?" she said before pushing the visor down, blocking her fiery grey eyes from my view before she turned to face forward again.

I tried to stop it, I really did and as I walked towards the bike and climbed onto it, I did a pretty convincing job but once I started the engine, I couldn't keep my lips from curling upward. I couldn't stop myself from grinning as she sat behind me, pissed off and stiff as a board, her hands gripping the seat below her for balance. She looked completely uncomfortable on my bike and for some reason that thought made my lips stretch even further. "You're going to want to hold on, Cupcake."

"I am holding on, Sugarplum."

I turned to grin at her over my shoulder, reaching behind me to guide her stiff arms. "To me, Nell. I don't want to go to jail if you fall off and die."

She snorted and struggled a bit as I forced her arms around my waist before letting go. I felt her start to remove them and chose that moment to rev the engine, lurching the bike forward making her arms tighten around me automatically. I grinned wider, feeling her front plant firmly against my back as I turned a corner a little too quickly. That grin remained planted on my face for the whole ride and perfect Nell Watson kept her arms around bad seed Grayson West the entire time.

Then we pulled up in front of her fucking mansion and faster than the blink of an eye, her arms were gone and she was standing next to the bike, her manicured fingers shifting over her dress, smoothing out the fabric compulsively even though it did nothing to get rid of the wrinkles.

My smile vanished as soon as she was no longer touching me, hating her all over again for acting like I was on fire now that we weren't moving. She pulled off the helmet, her hair tumbling over her shoulders in a way that made my fingers itch uncomfortably, making me curl them into fists, letting my anger overcome whatever soft feelings I was having towards her as she thrust the helmet at me.

My lip curled as I snatched it from her grasp. "Don't worry, Cupcake, poverty isn't catching. You're back in your pretty little world now and I'm pretty sure no one saw us. No one ever has to know that you went slumming. Your secret's safe with me."

Her gaze sharpened and her lips tightened into a thin line. "You're an asshole," she said through gritted teeth, turning her back on me, her spine ramrod straight as she walked away from me.

Something about the sight of her retreating form really pissed me off and I heard myself blurt, "What, no 'thank you'?" making her footsteps halt. I cursed myself for stopping her, logically knowing that the faster she walked away, the faster I could be at my house, warm in my bed, forgetting all about Nell Watson.

Instead, she turned towards me once more, her usual calm demeanor gone as she glared fiercely at me. "Thank you?" she spat, tilting her head back to give a short laugh. "Don't pretend like you don't get a sick sense of satisfaction from messing with me, Grayson. I never wanted your help so yeah, don't expect any 'thank you's."

Anger propelled me off my bike, making me stomp towards her quickly, invading her space within seconds. "You really need to be careful how you talk to me, Cupcake."

She tilted her head to the side and her voice was totally calm when she said. "I don't think so. I'm not afraid of you, Grayson West."

"Then the rumours must be true," I growled, knowing even as the words slipped out of my mouth that I was being a complete dick. "You really are crazy."

Just like that, she shut down. That angry light that had made her grey eyes almost glow in the dark vanished, her facial expression shifted and became a blank mask that gave away nothing. None of the starch left her spine but something in her stance shifted and she seemed a bit...smaller as she gave a casual shrug of her shoulders. "I guess so," she said, her voice dead as she turned her back on me once more.

"Shit," I muttered, running a hand through my hair before taking a step towards her but coming to a halt quickly, seeing that she'd already made it to the front door and was stepping over the threshold.

"Shit," I repeated when the door shut with a click behind her, leaving me standing on the cobblestone driveway feeling like a total asshole and probably looking like a criminal loitering there in the middle of the night.

After a minute I forced myself to move, to swing my leg over my bike and start it up, glancing back at the house only once before I took off.

The whole ride home I couldn't stop thinking about the look on her face when I'd called her crazy. I definitely preferred her angry glare to that weird, blank look she'd given me.

By the time I got home, I'd mulled it over and decided to put it behind me. What did I care what she thought of me, anyway? So what if I hurt her feelings? She'd get over it.

I'd just forget about her.

Chapter 3

Grayson's POV

"I'm telling you man, she's gorgeous."

"Uh huh," I said, not really paying attention to my buddy, Dan Eastwood as he talked about the car he was currently drooling over.

"I'm serious, Gray, she's unlike anything you've ever seen. I mean, she has a few issues, okay a lot of issues, but Frankie said I could use the garage after hours and work on her. I'm close too, man. I almost have the cash. A couple more shifts at the garage and she'll be all mine."

"Nice," I said, my eyes scanning the parking lot again. "What time is it?"

"Dude, are you even paying any attention to what I'm saying?" Dan said, crossing his arms over his chest and glaring at me.

I quirked an eyebrow at him, smirking at his offended expression. "Are you pouting right now, Dan?" I asked, punching him in the arm, dodging when he immediately retaliated. "Am I not giving you enough attention? I'm sorry, baby."

"Shut the fuck up, man," Dan growled, lunging at me, fists raised. He threw a few punches but I dodged easily. Dan was big and muscle bound but he wasn't the most agile guy. If he caught you though, he could pack a damn good punch. I'd ended up on my ass more than a few times thanks to Dan's meaty fists.

"Okay, okay, truce," I said, holding my hands up in surrender, waiting until Dan dropped his fists before letting my own hands fall to my sides, digging into my pocket for my cell phone. I frowned at the time. The bell was going to ring any minute now.

"What's up with you today, Gray? You seem…weird."

"Nothing," I said, hearing the irritation in my own voice as I scanned the parking lot once more, scowling when I still didn't see her anywhere. Was she skipping? She never skipped.

I looked down at my phone again, gritting my teeth at the hour, telling myself to just give up when the sound of crunching gravel caught my attention. My eyes narrowed on the BMW practically burning rubber through the parking lot as it pulled into a spot near the front of the school, close to where Dan and I were standing.

Nell's sister and her idiot boyfriend got out first and I gritted my teeth when Paige slammed her door with Nell still in the backseat of the two door car. Brian moved around the car and I heard Paige squeal as she launched herself at him, wrapping her legs around his waist and giggling as they proceeded to have a serious PDA session.

My gaze moved back to the car, watching Nell as she tried to balance her bag and a few books while getting out of the car, her expression pinched as she slammed the door and looked at the small watch on her wrist.

"We're going to be late," Nell said, her voice soft, timid as she tried to get her sister's attention.

The two lovebirds pulled apart and Brian grinned. "Let's skip, babe. I don't feel like putting up with all the bullshit today."

Paige's grin widened as she nodded and Nell frowned. "Paige, you already skipped the last two days."

"What are you, my mom?" Paige snapped, glaring over her shoulder at her sister. "Just fuck off, will you? You're going to be late, Nell. What are you going to do if you're perfect record is tarnished?" She gave a fake gasp and covered her mouth before tilting her head back and giggling in a way that sounded like nails on a chalkboard to me. Brian gave a few chuckles too before setting Paige down, slapping her on the ass as she climbed back into the car.

Nell started to move towards the school, her head down as she rushed forward, but Brian gripped her wrist, stopping her. "You could come too, Nell," he said, his lips twisting into a smirk that made my eyes narrow. Nell shook her head and tried to pull her arm away, but he wasn't letting go. My hands fisted and I took a step towards them without thinking about it. "C'mon, Nell," Brian said, leaning in closer to her making her back stiffen. Her expression changed as he spoke to her and I watched as all the colour drained from her skin, her grey eyes widening as she renewed her efforts to get away from him.

He pulled back slightly, using his free hand to run a finger down her cheek, his smirk becoming more smug and before I knew it, I was right there, my hand on his wrist, squeezing hard until I felt the bones grinding together a little and he was forced to let her go.

"What the fuck, man?" Brian snarled, pulling his wrist from my hand and glaring at me.

"Don't touch her," I snapped, rage boiling through me, taking me by surprise by its strength but I didn't stop to question it.

Brian stepped back and chuckled obnoxiously, looking over at Nell with a condescending expression that made me want to smack him. "Did you get yourself a bodyguard, Nell? Too pathetic to fight your own battles, is that it?"

My knuckles cracked as I fisted my hands at my sides, my vision going a little red at the insult. What the fuck was this guy's problem?

"We both know I'm not the pathetic one, Brian," Nell said, her voice quiet but calm and I watched as Brian's expression clouded with rage before he turned on his heel and stomped to the driver's side of the car. He peeled out of the parking lot, shoving his hand out the window and giving us the finger as he drove away.

I cleared my throat once the vehicle was out of sight and opened my mouth to talk to Nell but when I looked beside me, she was gone. My mouth snapped shut as I looked up towards the school, seeing her retreating form a few yards in front of me.

I frowned, telling myself that it wasn't worth it. Why should I chase after her when clearly, she didn't want to be chased?

My legs seemed to have other ideas though, and before I knew it, I was jogging to catch up to her.

"Ne——"

"Gray!" Dan cut me off, his big hand wrapping around my forearm, stopping me just before I reached her. "What are you doing, man? Did you nearly get into a fight with Brian Carr or was I imagining things?" I ground my teeth together, watching as Nell disappeared inside of the school. "Was it because of her? Is that why you're weird today?" He snorted as my eyes swung to him and narrowed. "Seriously dude, don't waste your time on that one. She's a few fries short of a happy meal. I see her at lunch sometimes and the chick organizes her food before she eats it." He tilted his head back and chuckled lightly making my teeth grind together harder. "No joke, she's nuts. You should think about Celine. She wants you, man," Dan finished, nudging me in the ribs with his elbow, his eyes finally connecting with mine fully and the humour in his gaze faded. "Hey, what's going on with you?"

I shook my head, trying to figure that out for myself. "I don't know, man I just…" I gave my head another shake, stepping towards the school to follow after Nell. "Just don't talk about her like that, alright?" I said over my shoulder, pushing the door open and scanning the nearly empty hallways, searching for her familiar light brown hair pulled back into a severe bun at the nape of her neck.

I walked quickly, vaguely registering the way people were moving out of my way, a hint of fear on their faces as I brushed past them. I ignored them all, focused on finding Nell, on telling her what had been keeping me up all night and driving me nuts since she walked away from me outside of her house with that dead look in her eyes.

I turned a corner and spotted her standing in front of her locker, spinning her combination with shaking fingers, her eyes darting up to look at the clock on the wall every five seconds.

"Hey," I said, giving a casual grin as I leaned a shoulder against the locker next to hers.

A muscle in her jaw jumped and I got the distinct impression she was gritting her teeth but she didn't even bother to glance at me.

My eyes narrowed. "I'm talking to you, Cupcake," I said, my voice pitched lower than it had been, sounding far less friendly.

"I'm going to be late," she said, her voice breathless with relief as she finally managed to get her locker open.

"I'll be quick," I snapped, getting angrier by the minute. She couldn't even fucking look at me? She'd looked at that Brian asshole no problem. "I just wanted to say——"

"Look, Grayson," she began, banging her fist on the locker next to her, her breath coming in fast pants as she glanced up at the clock again before lowering her hands to wipe her palms on her jeans, still not looking at me. "I don't have time to stand here and listen to you insult me, okay? I have to get to class."

I leaned my head back and focused on breathing slowly through my nose, calming the irritation that was quickly morphing into something closer to anger. "I said it'll only take a second, Cupcake." I ground out, leaning closer to her and as soon as her hands were out of the way, I reached over and slammed her locker door shut, reaching out to grip her chin and forcing her to meet my gaze.

I opened my mouth to speak but the look on her face made the words freeze in my throat. Her eyes were wide open, panic shining from their grey depths. Her skin was so pale it looked translucent and her lips were trembling with each short gasp of breath she took. "Hey," I said softly, frowning down at her, "are you going to pass out, Cupcake?"

For a second, she seemed to stop breathing and her eyes narrowed moments before some of the colour returned to her cheeks. "My name is not Cupcake," she hissed, her hand coming up to wrap around my wrist, pulling my fingers away from her chin. "Listen Grayson, you might not give a shit about whether you pass or fail but I do so I need to get to class. Why don't you run along and go do whatever you had planned for the day, okay?"

I glared at her profile as she spun her locker combination once more, jerking the door open hard enough to make it slam against the locker next to it as she quickly gathered what she needed for her class. For a long beat, I was so pissed at her that I couldn't even form words past the knot of rage in my throat. Why had I been so concerned about an apology, anyway? This chick didn't give a shit about what I had to say. She thought I was such a loser that she couldn't even stand to look me in the eye.

My teeth were grinding together so hard as I watched her slam her locker and walk away from me that I thought I might have chipped a few molars. I didn't take my eyes off her until she rounded a corner and disappeared and even the fact that she was no longer in my sight pissed me off.

Anger made my steps sharp, my boots slamming hard against the linoleum as I hurried to catch up to her, rounding the corner shortly after her. I caught up to her just as she opened the door to her class and took her first step inside. I stopped her by wrapping my hand around her bicep and pulling her towards me, forcing her back flush against my front as I leaned down slightly, my lips close to her ear as I whispered, "You think you know me, Cupcake?"

"N——"

"Shh," I whispered in her ear, my eyes connecting with a guy in the classroom. I think his name was Craig and he looked like he was ready to jump up from his seat to protect little Nell. My eyes narrowed and I gave him a look that had frightened far bigger men and his face went a little white as he sank further into his chair. My lips stretched into a smug grin as I let my hand drift up over Nell's shoulder, making sure she couldn't get out of my grip without causing a scene. "You think you're so much better than me, that you're too perfect to even talk to me? I was feeling bad about the way I talked to you last night but I can see now that I shouldn't have bothered. I could've left you there last night, I could've driven right by you but I didn't. No matter what you think about me, that deserves a bit of respect, wouldn't you agree?" The bell rang and I could feel the way her whole body shook. Was she starting to get the message? Did she understand now that no one talked to me like that and got away with it? "Better go, Nell," I said, spitting out her name like it tasted bad. "I wouldn't want you to be late for class."

My hand slid slowly off her trembling shoulder and I pulled my body away from hers inch by inch, revelling in the feel of her shivers as they raced all through her. She was terrified, so scared that she shook with it. This I got, this I understood. I knew all about fear and making people feel this way about me. I should just stick to what I know and forget about apologizing for stupid shit that I shouldn't even feel bad for.

Yeah, I thought, a smirk spreading across my lips as I took two steps back, letting her go completely, this works for me.

I was just about to turn my back on her and walk away when she looked at me over her shoulder and something in her eyes made me stop dead in my tracks. She was pale white again, her grey eyes wide with emotions that skittered across her gaze frantically. For a second, I was caught by that look in her eyes, trying to figure out exactly what I was seeing. Out of all the emotions darting across her features there was one that wasn't there, one that I had expected, even looked forward to seeing.

Fear.

She's not afraid of me.

I blinked when she tore her gaze from mine and faced forward, that Craig guy now standing in front of her, talking to her quietly while darting glances at me, his eyes narrowed. I curled my lip at him and turned on my heel, walking away from Nell Watson and resolving not to think about her again. What did it matter if she wasn't afraid of me or if she was? She wasn't my problem.

Nell's POV

Nothing had changed.

Everything was exactly as it had been the day before regardless of whatever pacts I'd made to myself. I still sat through my classes with my back ramrod straight, my notes meticulous and colour coded, my pens and pencils lined up perfectly across my desk. Hadn't I told myself I'd stop caring? Didn't I say I'd focus on what I wanted for once?

Frustrated, I reached out and pushed at my pens, sending them into disarray across my desk, hating the way my heart rate kicked up a few notches and my palms went damp at the sight of them.

Pathetic. I couldn't even take a stand against my writing utensils. How the hell had I expected myself to stand up to my parents?

Last night, with alcohol coursing through my veins, I'd felt brave for once, I'd felt like a different person who wasn't so scared of stepping out of line. But when I woke up this morning...all I had to show for it was a headache.

That damn coil in my chest was back in full force and despite the conversation I'd had with Eleanor at the Johnston's party, I still couldn't stand the thought of disappointing her even though my very existence seemed to do just that.

So she was back, that pathetic Nell who wasn't drunk, who couldn't take on anyone, who was going to continue to work her ass off to prove herself to people who would never give their approval.

And that other Nell, the one who didn't care, who wasn't so afraid, well, she seemed to only come out when Grayson West was around.

I winced at the thought of him, remembering the way his fingers had clenched in anger as he'd held me against him, my back to his front, his words in my ear making shame wind through me. That's what I got for losing control. With anyone else, I thought so hard about what I was going to say that I usually didn't even speak but with him...

With him the words just came tumbling out. I didn't even have a chance to second guess them before they were in the air and mortally offending the most dangerous guy in school.

I needed to apologize to him, to explain…

What? That I was so focused on getting to class on time that I would've said anything to get him out of my way? Should I tell him that the coil in my chest had been winding tight ever since that morning, that when Brian grabbed me outside of his car and whispered…what he whispered in my ear it had gotten to the point where I thought that coil might snap and by the time I got to my locker, it only felt tighter every second that brought me closer to being late for class?

I gritted my teeth and watched the teacher jot a few things on the board without really paying attention, letting my mind wander, replaying the words he'd whispered in my ear.

You think you know me, Cupcake?

No. I had no idea who Grayson West was. I only knew what people thought of him. People were scared of him. Other students moved out of his way when they saw him coming and I didn't miss the way Craig had fallen back into his seat when he'd made eye contact with Grayson. They thought he was dangerous and maybe they were right.

But…

He didn't have to stop last night. He didn't have to pull over and give me a ride home but he did, and as irritating as he could be, he hadn't been wrong when he'd insinuated that I should've been thanking him rather than snapping at him.

Then he'd come up to me today and I couldn't think past the second hand on the clock ticking away and I was rude to him again.

I closed my eyes and let out a slow breath, frustrated with my lack of control around him. What was it about him that made me lose it?

I opened my eyes again and focused resolutely on the teacher as she told us to open our books and do the practice questions. I sighed and looked down at my paper, reaching for one of my pencils before my hand froze.

They were all perfectly organized again, not a single pen or pencil out of place.

I wanted to laugh, to tilt my head back and give in to the helpless feeling welling up inside of me. How was I supposed to let go of everything I'd worked so hard for when I couldn't even handle having disorganized pencils for five minutes?

"So Nell, how are you today?" Dr. Sylvia Brown asked me, her light blue eyes peering at me over a pair of reading glasses that I suspected were just for show.

"Fine," I muttered, sinking further into my chair, sitting on my hands to keep them from curling into the fabric of my shirt. She always wrote notes when I did that.

Her gaze followed my arms to where they disappeared beneath me and her pen scratched across the yellow pad in her lap for a moment before she focused on me again with that bland smile she always wore during our sessions.

"I saw your report card. Your grades are excellent. All your teachers think you're an exceptionally hard worker and considering your extra-curriculars, you have a very good chance of being admitted to any university you want next year." She paused for a second and I nodded, not sure what she wanted me to say. I hated this game, trying to figure out what I should say to make me seem more normal, worrying that I'd let something slip that would show my crazy. "Is that what you want, Nell?"

My eyes shot to hers, my brows lowering as I tried to figure out what she was asking me. "What do you mean?" I asked, my voice coming out a little breathless as my heart beat hard in my chest.

"I mean, Nell, all this work you've been doing, all this time you've spent on getting these grades, it's obvious that you're working towards something, that you have a specific goal in mind and I think that's great." I nodded again, frowning harder trying to figure out where she was going with this. She cleared her throat and just stared at me for a long beat before she glanced down at a piece of paper in her lap. "Your mother called this morning." I straightened in my seat, everything inside of me going still as she slowly raised her eyes to give me a stern look. "She thinks you're not taking your medication. She said you've been acting out lately and she's worried about you."

Acid burned up my throat and my lungs lay useless in my chest as all the oxygen left the room.

"Nell, we're trying to help you, do you understand that?"

I nodded, tucking my chin closer to my chest, wishing my hair was untied so it could cover my face which was probably red and blotchy from not breathing.

"I'm going to prescribe you something new," Sylvia said softly and I watched as her long fingers worked to grip her pen before scrawling something across a small slip of paper. She held it out to me once she was finished and I had to lift my weight from my hands in order to reach out and grab it.

When my fingers were about to close on the paper, she pulled it back. "Promise me you'll take it, Nell."

My eyes met hers squarely and for the first time since the session began, breathing came easy and that coil in my chest wasn't quite so irritating. "I promise," I said, the lie slipping easily from my lips as I took the paper from her and tucked it into my bag.

"Great," she said, her tone a bit smug as she smiled at me and reached over to pat my arm but her hand was cold and the move was less than comforting. I smiled back anyway, recognizing my cue.

The rest of the session passed quickly and when I stood to leave, I caught that satisfied look on her face again. She thought she won. She thought she got to me, that she'd managed to heal me, even just a little bit.

She was wrong.

I walked out of the room, barely even noticing the girls standing nearby, whispering behind their hands as they stared at me and laughed. I felt a glimmer of that numbness I'd felt the night before steal over me, making me not care quite so much that my sessions were held at lunch every Thursday, that they had to be at the school where anyone could see me walk into the counsellors office once a week.

Your mother called this morning.

I gritted my teeth hard, bumping into someone without really noticing as the hallway seemed to close in on me, my breathing coming in ragged little pants that sounded unhealthy to my own ears. I was acting out? Why, because I'd shown up to that party? Now she wanted me to be even more heavily medicated?

I let out a short, breathless laugh that was barely above a whisper.

Joke's on her, I thought, lifting my fingers to rub the tender spot on my forehead where a throbbing pain was just beginning. I hadn't been taking pills since the summer. I'd been keeping track diligently, flushing the correct dosage down the toilet each morning, feeding the sewer rats the drugs that I hated.

I'd just add the new one to the mix.

God, I need air.

My lungs strained against my ribs, burning for oxygen but the recycled air in the hallway just wasn't cutting it. I needed out.

With hurried steps, I made it to the end of the hallway and slammed into a pair of double doors that took me outside. I gasped a few, long breaths of the crisp air, my eyes watering as it burnt its way down my throat and into my starved lungs.

I was walking towards my car, my knees shaking with each step and I was nearly there when something in the corner of my eye made me stop. I blinked a couple of times, turning my head slightly so I could look at the bike more fully. There it was, that horrible machine that had brought me home the night before, endangering my life with each turn of a corner. That damn bike had terrified me from the second I saw it pull up next to me and I never ever planned on getting on it until Grayson egged me on which was around the time when I lost all semblance of reason.

A part of me couldn't believe I'd done it, even as I'd climbed onto the death trap but another part of me revelled in it.

That part of me, the part that only came out when we'd started moving and the cold wind had whipped against my skin until I couldn't feel it anymore, that part of me hadn't been scared at all. That part of me had loved being on that bike.

For a few minutes the night before, I felt like I was moving towards something that had absolutely nothing to do with the family that despised me or the students that whispered about me...

For a minute, I considered never getting off that bike.

So when we'd stopped outside of my house and the world came crashing down around me once more, I got away as fast as I could, hating that bike and its driver for making me think, even for a second, that I could escape only to be brought right back to the mouth of the beast.

A prickle at my neck had me shifting my gaze towards the school where the picnic benches were and there he was, Grayson West surrounded by friends, a girl with long red hair hanging off of him as he stared at me with narrowed eyes.

I could've left you there last night.

Why didn't he? Why didn't he drive by when he clearly hated me? Why did he stop for someone who'd been nothing but rude to him?

I didn't break eye contact with him, not even when the red head leaned into him and whispered something in his ear making him tilt his head slightly but even as he listened, he kept his eyes on mine. I should've walked over there and apologize to him, told him I appreciated it, that I overreacted that morning and because he was who he was, I'd snapped at him.

Too bad my feet seemed to be super-glued to the spot.

"Nell?"

I blinked, breaking eye contact with Grayson to look to my left where Craig was standing, his forehead wrinkled as he looked at me with concern. "You okay?" he asked, reaching out to gently wrap his fingers around my bicep. I smiled up at him a little stiffly, trying to tell myself that I didn't find his touch uncomfortable.

"I'm fine," I said, wishing my voice hadn't come out quite so breathless. "Just getting some air."

He nodded, his eyes roving over my features, his forehead still wrinkled as he examined me. "You look pale."

I shrugged. "Just tired."

He nodded again. "What did you do to get on Grayson West's bad side, anyway?" he asked after a beat of silence.

"What do you mean?" I asked, resisting the urge to look over at Grayson again.

"I mean, he can't seem to stop glaring at you and he followed you to class this morning. It was…weird, Nell. You should try to steer clear of him. He's dangerous."

I frowned, my eyes falling to Craig's chest. "I was rude to him."

Craig chuckled lightly, using his grip on my arm to start steering us towards the school, his body blocking my view of Grayson but somehow, I still felt the weight of his gaze on me. "That doesn't sound like you, Nell."

I shrugged, not knowing what to say to that. It didn't sound like me but every time Grayson showed his face in front of me, I forgot all about the control I prided myself on.

"Anyway, I think you should stick with me in the hallways from now on. I don't want you having any run-ins with a guy like that on your own."

"You don't have to protect me, Craig," I said quietly, walking into the school ahead of him.

"Yeah well, Brian doesn't want my help so I figured I might as well expend my energies elsewhere."

The strain in his voice made my heart clench and without thinking, I reached over and rested my hand on his forearm. "You haven't given up on him. Maybe one day he'll be able to appreciate that."

Craig's eyes softened as he looked down at me and a small smile curved his lips. "Maybe. Until then, I'll be keeping an eye on you, okay?"

I shrugged and faced forward once more, taking my hand away from Craig and tucking it into my pocket. I wanted to argue with him, to tell him that I'd be fine, that he could focus on anything else but I didn't have a solid argument for why he didn't need to worry. I mean, I'd offended Grayson more than a couple of times and considering his reputation, I should be scared.

Only...

No matter what the rumours were about him, no matter how angry his glares were, I just didn't think he would hurt me.

Ever.

As we walked into the school, I frowned at my own logic. Maybe I really was crazy because despite the fact that I'd seen him beat the shit out of someone else before, I couldn't seem to get it out of my brain that he wasn't exactly the woman beating type.

Maybe it had been the way he'd gripped Brian's wrist that morning, squeezing until my hand was free. For a long beat I'd just stood there and stared up at him as he glared at Brian, my eyes caught on the hard angle of his jaw and the anger darkening his features. He'd been truly angry at Brian on my behalf and considering the fact that we could barely tolerate each other, Grayson's protective attitude had confused the shit out of me.

Was he just trying his hand at being nice to the crazy chick or was it something else?

I shook my head as we stopped outside of my classroom and Craig gave me a friendly wave before walking away. I needed to focus. I needed to stop thinking about Grayson West but there was the small matter of the guilt that had wound its spindly fingers around my consciousness. I'd been rude to him, unforgivably so considering how he'd been decent to me.

Taking a seat at my desk, I set my notebook in front of me and hatched a plan. The next time I saw Grayson West, I'd simply walk up to him and offer him an apology. I'd keep it short and to the point and then I'd walk away and forget about him for good.

"Excuse me, miss? This isn't what I ordered."

I wiped my sweaty palms on the brown apron employees at The Bean had to wear. "I'm sorry," I mumbled, taking the man's coffee from him and setting it aside, starting a new one. I frowned as I worked, thinking over the first one I'd made. It had been right, I was sure of it.

Whatever, I'd just make it better this time. "Here you go, sir. Large chai vanilla latte made with soy milk," I said, handing it to the man who just nodded at me as he answered his phone.

I ignored the anger burning in my belly as the man walked away without a word of thanks, turning instead to the woman waiting to place her order next.

I was ringing up her purchase when a coffee was suddenly slammed onto the counter in front of me, some of the contents spilling out of the opening at the top and splashing my arm, making me jump back.

"It's still not right," the man from earlier snarled, his eyes narrowing at me in accusation.

"I-I-I'm sorry," I stammered, my heart beating a furious tattoo in my chest as I looked away from his angry eyes, feeling the weight of everyone's gaze who was standing in line or was near enough to hear the man.

I immediately started working on a new coffee, my hands shaking so hard that I nearly dropped the cup but I managed to finish it without incident, putting a lid on it and handing it to the man just as his phone started ringing again.

He glared at me as he answered the phone, his free hand shooting out to grab the cup but his aim was off and he knocked the cup from my hand instead, making its contents spill all over the counter and down the front of his shirt. "Jesus Christ!" he shouted, holding his arms out to his sides as he stared down at the mess on his expensive looking clothes. "What are you, some kind of idiot?" he snapped, his face a mask of fury as he glared at me, grabbing a nearby stack of napkins and trying to sop up some of the liquid that would probably irreparably stain his shirt.

"N-n-n..." I stuttered, my breath coming in short, breathy gasps as I tried to get my racing heart to calm down but my nerves were shot and I could feel the panic closing in on me.

Oh god, oh no, please not now.

The edges of my vision went grey and the sound of the man's voice was muffled now as he continued to curse at me, calling me names and asking to speak to my manager.

I couldn't focus, couldn't speak, couldn't even move as he leaned further over the counter, bringing his face closer to mine as I stood there blinking at him.

"Hello?" he said, waving a hand in front of my face. "Jesus, no wonder you can't make a coffee. Are you on drugs? Where's your manager?"

"Is there a problem?" Art, the general manager said, suddenly standing next to me.

"Yeah, there's a problem," the customer said. "This girl made my coffee wrong twice and when she made it again for the third time she spilled it all over me. Is it your policy to hire incompetent employees?"

My eyelid twitched as Art offered the man an apology and with their focus being away from me for a second, I managed to get in a few solid breaths, some of the fog receding from my vision enough for me to start on another new coffee for the man.

"I'm sorry," I muttered as I made it, not sure if I was apologizing to Art or to the asshole with the dirty shirt but it didn't matter.

My hands were shaking almost uncontrollably but somehow I managed to finish the coffee, holding it out carefully to the customer who just sneered down at it. "Are you serious?" he asked, curling his lip in disgust. His eyes shifted to Art and he lifted his hand to point a finger in his face. "You'd better watch your employees. I'll bet you any money this one got high before work. You can see it in her eyes," he said sliding his gaze over to me once more before heading into the restroom to clean himself up a bit.

I pressed a hand to my chest, the coil that lived there wound so tight that it physically hurt with every beat of my heart. My head ached and my breathing was still erratic but the line-up was getting long now that the man had left and I tried to focus enough to serve the next customer.

"Tommy will get them," Art said, gesturing to Tommy who'd been bussing tables but came rushing over to serve the customers as Art grabbed my arm and dragged me through the swinging door to the back room.

"I'm not on drugs," I blurted, hating how reed thin my voice was.

He waved a dismissive hand and relief made it slightly easier to breathe. I blinked, realizing I was still holding the fourth cup of coffee that the man had refused to take. I looked around for the garbage but Art's voice stopped me. "I'm going to have to let you go, Nell."

I froze, my ears buzzing as I replayed his words over and over again, sure I'd heard him wrong. "What?" I whispered.

"I can't keep you on anymore, Nell."

Stricken, I looked up at him, the panic that had been receding, doubling as his words registered. "You're firing me?" I croaked, my free hand groping for the counter behind me, my knees starting to shake from the effort of standing up. "B-b-but I made the right coffee. I swear."

"It's not about the coffee, Nell. Sometimes you get shitty customers and you have to be able to deal with them. You're good at this job but sometimes you're so focused on getting everything perfect that when something goes wrong you lose it." He shook his head and may have muttered an apology but the ringing in my ears drowned him out. "...your time, okay? Don't worry...shift...covered...cheque next week."

What? What was he saying? I nodded anyway, not really caring that I hadn't heard him. What did it matter? I was fired.

I'd gotten fired.

"Oh my god," I muttered, my throat closing in panic as I thought about college applications. What if they wanted to use this as a reference and I had to tell them I got fired? I had written about my job on my applications so they might ask me about it. If I couldn't even handle a job at The Bean, how the hell would I be able to handle a full college workload and extra curriculars? They'd reject me for sure.

I made an odd gurgling sound, my eyes shooting all around me, searching for an escape, only half noticing that Art wasn't there anymore and probably hadn't been for a while.

Tripping over my own feet, I stumbled out the back door, my lungs aching with the need to breathe, my ears still ringing as the panic refused to release its hold on me. I leaned back against the wall, sliding down until my ass landed on the dirty pavement next to the dumpster out back.

What was I going to do?

I could try to get my job back. I could promise them I'd do better, that I wouldn't make any more mistakes ever. They'd take me back if I begged, right?

Even as a part of me resigned myself to grovelling, another part rebelled at the thought. Jeez, was I that pathetic? Would I seriously beg for my shitty job back?

Yes.

I would. I really would. The thought of people knowing I'd been fired, of my family knowing, made my heart race anew. Eleanor would give me one of those looks tinged with disappointment and disgust, like she couldn't believe she'd raised someone like me. Dean would look down his nose at me like he'd expected it all along, like he wasn't really surprised that I was letting him down again.

And Paige...

She'd laugh at me.

I flinched at the thought, my wide eyes searching the nearly empty section of the parking lot for answers but none came.

I blinked when I saw someone walking towards the lone car parked at the rear of the building. It was the guy from earlier, the asshole customer who probably hadn't even realized what he'd ordered because those coffees had been perfect. I never messed up. He was walking to his fancy car with a long, angry stride, shouting into his phone, clearly describing his trip to The Bean and how he'd run into a drugged up server who couldn't get his order right. My eyes narrowed and my hands tightened into fists only my left hand was hampered by something.

I looked down to see myself still holding that damn coffee cup, the one I'd made as a last ditch effort to appease the man, the one he'd looked at with disgust.

Slowly, I looked from the coffee to the guy as he unlocked his car and opened the door.

My heart pounded so hard it felt like it was coming out of my chest but that panic that had been choking me receded as I scrambled to my feet and walked a few steps closer to that man and his car. I gritted my teeth, quirking an eyebrow as I read his license plate: IL SUE U.

Okay, safe to say this guy was a dick.

He started his expensive car and the quiet purr of the engine only served to piss me off even further. He'd cost me my job and since I was already fired, why shouldn't I chuck his stupid soy vanilla chai latte at his overpriced car?

My lips twitched into a smile as I stopped and pulled my arm back just as he put his car into gear.

Not yet.

I waited until he pulled a little closer, not even caring that he could see me, my heart hammering hard in my chest as a warm feeling of exhilaration pulsed through my veins. I could do this. I could show him that I wasn't

I made an odd gurgling sound, my eyes shooting all around me, searching for an escape, only half noticing that Art wasn't there anymore and probably hadn't been for a while.

Tripping over my own feet, I stumbled out the back door, my lungs aching with the need to breathe, my ears still ringing as the panic refused to release its hold on me. I leaned back against the wall, sliding down until my ass landed on the dirty pavement next to the dumpster out back.

What was I going to do?

I could try to get my job back. I could promise them I'd do better, that I wouldn't make any more mistakes ever. They'd take me back if I begged, right?

Even as a part of me resigned myself to grovelling, another part rebelled at the thought. Jeez, was I that pathetic? Would I seriously beg for my shitty job back?

Yes.

I would. I really would. The thought of people knowing I'd been fired, of my family knowing, made my heart race anew. Eleanor would give me one of those looks tinged with disappointment and disgust, like she couldn't believe she'd raised someone like me. Dean would look down his nose at me like he'd expected it all along, like he wasn't really surprised that I was letting him down again.

And Paige...

She'd laugh at me.

I flinched at the thought, my wide eyes searching the nearly empty section of the parking lot for answers but none came.

I blinked when I saw someone walking towards the lone car parked at the rear of the building. It was the guy from earlier, the asshole customer who probably hadn't even realized what he'd ordered because those coffees had been perfect. I never messed up. He was walking to his fancy car with a long, angry stride, shouting into his phone, clearly describing his trip to The Bean and how he'd run into a drugged up server who couldn't get his order right. My eyes narrowed and my hands tightened into fists only my left hand was hampered by something.

I looked down to see myself still holding that damn coffee cup, the one I'd made as a last ditch effort to appease the man, the one he'd looked at with disgust.

Slowly, I looked from the coffee to the guy as he unlocked his car and opened the door.

My heart pounded so hard it felt like it was coming out of my chest but that panic that had been choking me receded as I scrambled to my feet and walked a few steps closer to that man and his car. I gritted my teeth, quirking an eyebrow as I read his license plate: IL SUE U.

Okay, safe to say this guy was a dick.

He started his expensive car and the quiet purr of the engine only served to piss me off even further. He'd cost me my job and since I was already fired, why shouldn't I chuck his stupid soy vanilla chai latte at his overpriced car?

My lips twitched into a smile as I stopped and pulled my arm back just as he put his car into gear.

Not yet.

I waited until he pulled a little closer, not even caring that he could see me, my heart hammering hard in my chest as a warm feeling of exhilaration pulsed through my veins. I could do this. I could show him that I wasn't some dumb pushover, that just because he had money didn't mean he could walk all over people.

Now.

The timing was perfect. I had a clear shot and he wasn't even looking in my direction, too busy on the phone again.

I pulled my arm back a bit further, lining up the throw and then...

I froze. Just like that, all that determination waned out of me, leaving behind that annoying panic that I just couldn't shake. The car sped off and my shoulders slumped knowing I'd missed my chance, feeling far more disappointed in myself than the situation warranted.

Wasn't I going to take a stand? Wasn't I going to change?

I turned around and tossed the coffee into the large trash bin, feeling a headache beginning to pound at my temples.

Dread settled on my shoulders, weighing me down as I wondered if I'd ever be able to change, if I could ever get rid of that damn coil in my chest that ruled me. It wasn't just about the coffee. It was about Eleanor and that party, the pens on my desk, the new prescription from Sandra and the way I'd spoken to Grayson just because I might've been a minute late to class if I let him talk.

At the thought of Grayson, a slight smile curved my lips. He would've thrown the coffee. He definitely would've gone through with it.

Granted, he might've also dragged the guy out of his car and started beating the shit out of him but at least he wouldn't stand there, numb and petrified like I had done.

What would it be like to have people be scared of me when I walked down the hallways? How great would it feel if I could've made that guy back off with just a look the way Grayson had done with Craig the day before?

Maybe I should ask him to give me lessons.

I nearly laughed aloud at the thought. Like he'd waste his time on someone like me. He had better things to do than hang out with girls who were unhinged and couldn't seem to stop themselves from insulting him.

With a sigh, I walked towards my beat up little car, pausing beside my door as I caught sight of my own reflection. I was still wearing my stupid apron. Suddenly, it felt heavier, like it was weighing me down, reminding me of my failure and with shaking fingers, I struggled to undo the ties at my back before roughly yanking it over my head.

I held it out in front of me for a long moment, staring at the damn thing as if it were a cockroach rather than a harmless piece of material. Finally, I began to walk back towards the dumpster and without pausing, I chucked the stupid thing in the green bin along with the asshole's coffee.

My lips twitched as I strode back towards my car, my spine a little straighter as I brushed my hands on my pants as if the wipe away the remnants of the apron. There, that was impulsive, right? I could change if I wanted to. I didn't need lessons from Grayson or anyone else. I'd just stop caring what people thought of me so much, stop caring what my parents thought of me and I would most definitely stop caring about the shitty job I'd just lost.

I could do this.

I reached out to grip my door handle, my mouth still tilted up in the corners when I saw my reflection once more and paused. My hair was a mess. Taking the apron off had knocked my bun out of place and a few strands of hair had come loose, hanging around my face. My hands twitched at my sides, eager to smooth it back into place but I gritted my teeth against the urge, stepping into the car instead, cringing as the door screeched loudly until it was closed with me inside.

The car started on the third try but I didn't put it in drive. Instead, I sat there with my hands clenched on the steering wheel, staring at The Bean, feeling that panic creep up on me again. I got fired.

I wanted to climb into that dumpster and get my apron back. I wanted to talk to Art, to convince him that I was a good employee, that I never made the wrong coffee.

But more than any of that, I wanted to not care. I wanted to just shrug and drive away like it had been nothing.

With a sigh, I put my car into drive, looking both ways before pulling out and heading towards the road. When I stopped, waiting for a pause in traffic, I glanced in the review mirror and I watched as my face drained of colour.

Slowly, I lifted my shaking fingers to touch my perfectly smooth hair, feeling for the fly-aways that had been there moments before.

They were gone, all tucked neatly back into the bun like they'd never been there.

Clenching my hand into a fist, I banged it against the steering wheel, suddenly furious that I didn't even have control of my own hands let alone my life.

I wanted to mess it up again. I wanted to pull out my bun and run my fingers through it until it looked like I'd just rolled out of bed.

Instead, I waited for a break in traffic and pulled out onto the street.

I came awake with a gasp, my heart racing as my nightmare faded quickly, already forgetting what it was about. I winced, rubbing my head as I realized there was an odd ringing in my ears that wouldn't go away. Did I have a headache?

Oh wait, it was my phone.

Rushing to snatch it off my nightstand, I accidentally knocked it to the floor. Gritting my teeth, I flung back my sheets and stood, finally managing to wrap my hands around the device. "Hello?" I breathed into the receiver, my voice sounding like I'd been smoking two packs a day since I was eight.

"Nell?" Craig said, his voice raised over the sounds of a party.

"Craig. What's wrong?" I asked, straightening as my eyes adjusted to the dark room.

"Nell, I'm so sorry to call you like this but I..." he trailed off and sounds of groaning and what seemed like a struggle filled my ear. "Sorry," he mumbled after a moment. "Nell, it's Paige."

My heart stopped in my chest and my knees started to shake so hard that I had to sit. "Is she okay?" I whispered, my throat closing as fear crushed my lungs into dust.

"I...I think so?"

A muffled sob worked its way up my throat at the uncertainty in his tone. "Where are you?"

He rattled off an address on the other side of town and I was already moving before he was done, slipping on some clothes and grabbing my jacket and keys on my way out.

"What happened?" I croaked as I silently walked down the stairs, my footsteps muffled on the carpet.

"I don't know, Nell. I came with them but they slipped away from me for a while and when I found them, Brian was so drunk that he was throwing up all over himself and Paige was just...out. Everyone keeps telling me she's fine whenever I mention an ambulance. I just...should I call 911, Nell? I don't know what to do. Brian's a mess. I need to take him home but I can't just leave her."

"I'm coming," I said, already in my car, sending up a silent thank you when it started on the first try.

"Hurry up," Craig said, sounding like he was gritting his teeth and then he disconnected.

"Oh my god," I whispered, taking a corner way too fast as I pushed my rusty little car to the limit. What if she was overdosing? Everyone was saying she was fine but what did they know? Were they all doing the same shit she was? Oh god, what if she di——

No. Don't go there, Nell. Don't panic yet. Just...not yet.

I would've laughed if I had any breath left in my lungs. Panic was my middle name and I don't think I took a whole breath for the entire ride to the run down house across town.

Somehow, I managed to hold it together though, my eyes wide and my skin tingling weirdly from the adrenaline pumping through me at the moment. I had to find her.

I burst into the house without knocking, not even caring that people gave me dirty looks as I bolted inside, frantically searching for Paige.

"Nell!" My gaze locked on Craig, his arm wrapped around Brian's waist, holding him up as he slumped against his friend.

"Where is she?" I shouted over the music, reaching out to grip a handful of Craig's t-shirt.

His eyes widened slightly but he nodded towards the stairs leading to the basement. "Down there."

I nodded and moved around him, fear clawing at me from the inside out, tearing my flesh but my racing heart was somehow holding me together, keeping me sane until I saw her, until I knew she was alright.

"I'm bringing Brian to my car, Nell!" I heard Craig call out from behind me and I just gave him a backwards wave, not even caring what he was saying. I just needed to find her.

Nobody spoke to me as I raced down the stairs and came to skidding halt at the bottom, my eyes scanning the area for my sister.

I spotted her on an old, worn out couch, her body slumped sideways, her head lolling on the armrest as the two people beside her shared a bong.

"Paige," I whispered, closing the distance between us and kneeling in front of her, my shaking hands fluttering over her face, not quite sure what to do. "Oh my god, Paige," I choked, my breath wheezing in and out of my lungs, my heartbeat so frantic that I thought I might pass out.

I pulled my phone out of my pocket and started to dial 911 when the girl next to Paige reached out and snatched it from my hand. "Don't even think about it, loser. She's fine. Just passed out."

"She is not fine," I snapped, ready to tackle the bitch to get my phone back.

The girl rolled her heavily black rimmed eyes at me and gave me a condescending look. "She took some pills and mixed it with booze. She was flying high for a bit but now she's passed out. Don't worry, she just needs to sleep it off."

"Give me my phone," I ground out, holding my hand out, palm up.

"Fine," the girl said, holding my phone just out of reach. "But just think about this for a second. She already hates you, right?" I frowned, realizing this girl knew who I was. "Let's just say you call an ambulance and the cops come too and this whole party gets busted. Do you really think Paige will appreciate your interference when all her friends hate her? And from what I know about mommy and daddy, my guess is they'd be pretty pissed if their daughter was brought into the hospital for drug use." She gave me a half smile and a shrug as she set the phone into my hand. "Think about it."

I stared at the phone in my hand, my head so mixed up that for a second, I didn't even know where I was.

Then Paige made a noise and everything became clear again.

"Paige," I whispered, my hands cupping her face, shaking her shoulders, pinching her skin, anything to get her eyes to open.

She flinched when I slapped her cheek lightly and her eyes opened as slit.

I breathed a shaky sigh of relief as she glared at me groggily. "Ffffug offff," she mumbled before her eyes closed again and she shifted sideways slightly, trying to get in a more comfortable position.

The girl next to her took a hit from the bong and grinned at me as she held the smoke inside. "Told you she was fine," she said, exhaling smoke at the same time.

I just shook my head, some of my panic fading but not enough. Not even close.

I needed to get her out of there.

Leaning forward, I wrapped my arms around her, trying to prop her up somehow so I could, I don't know, drag her out of there but she was dead weight and as soon as I let her go, she just slumped back against the couch.

I made a sound caught between a groan and a sob and moved forward to try again, freezing when my eyes fell on a pill bottle that had fallen out of her sweater pocket.

Slowly, my hand shifted and my fingers wrapped around the prescription bottle, pulling it close to my face to read the label, already knowing what it would say.

It was mine.

I read my name on the label again and again, refusing to believe that she'd be that stupid. Did she even know what this stuff did? Did she have any idea what mixing it with alcohol could've done? If she had taken too much…

My hand began to shake and I gripped the bottle hard enough that the plastic felt like it might break at any moment.

I stared down at my younger sister and for that one moment, there was no panic. Nope. For one, drawn out moment, I was a sea of calm and Paige was just…no one. Paige was just some girl I didn't recognize, passed out at a party that I should never have come to. The Paige I knew wouldn't have been so stupid. The Paige I grew up with wasn't so blind that she would think taking these fucking pills would make her happy. No, this girl was someone else.

"Hey, is there any beer down he——"

I stiffened at the sound of his voice, recognizing him without turning around to face the stairs he'd obviously just come down.

I froze, my calm vanishing in the space of an instant and for the life of me, I couldn't seem to move. Why was it that he always saw me like this? What was it about Grayson West that made him show up whenever I really didn't want him to?

"Cupcake?" he said, his tone laced with a mix of disdain and humour as he stepped up beside me, crossing his arms over his chest as he stared down at me. "What the hell are you doing down here, Cupcake?"

I gritted my teeth, refusing to look at him as he called me that stupid name. I just shook my head and mentally willed my sister to wake up enough for us to walk out of there.

She started snoring.

"Looks like your sister had a good night," Grayson said, his voice a little softer now, a little closer to me and I watched from the corner of my eye as he reached out to rest his hand on my shoulder, turning me to face him. "Did you?" he asked as he pushed my shoulders until our bodies were square. Still, I refused to look him in the eye, keeping my gaze somewhere around his collarbone, wishing he'd just go away so I could figure this shitty night out and go home. "You drunk again, Cupcake?" he asked, slowly shifting a hand to my jaw, using his fingers to push my face upward, forcing me to meet his eyes.

I ground my teeth together, ready to snap at him, ready to lurch away from his touch but as soon as our gazes connected, I froze.

I'd expected him to be laughing at me. I'd expected him to crack some joke, to make fun of me for the way I'd acted the other night but instead, his dark brown eyes were looking into mine steadily, his lips pressed into a thin line and his brow furrowed in…

Concern.

I frowned, silent for a long beat before I opened my mouth to respond.

Only I didn't get the chance because a guy's loud voice interrupted. "C'mon West. Get a move on with those beers. We're thirsty!" His voice was loud and his footsteps were louder as he pounded his way down the stairs, halting at the bottom, his wide eyes caught on Grayson and me standing close together, one of his hands on my shoulder and the other one under my jaw.

I jerked back as Grayson looked over at his friend, putting some distance between the two of us just as the other guy came rushing over and flung his arm around Grayson.

"Dude, you should've told me you were coming down here to meet a chick. Is that why you've been denying Celine all night?"

Grayson barred his teeth at his friend and made a noise that would've had me backing up ten paces if it was directed at me.

The guy just ignored him and turned his grin on me. "You're Nell, right?" he said, sticking out his hand for me to shake, unbothered when Grayson shrugged until his friend removed his arm. "I'm Dan."

I blinked and before I could move, Dan had shifted closer to me, gripping my hand where it was hanging at my side and pumping it a couple of times in his meaty fist.

I gave him a wary look, pulling my hand from his and taking a small step back, not wanting to step on the two stoner's toes.

"Did you just get here?" Dan said, not noticing my retreat as he kept looking at me with a wide grin on his handsome face. He was so big that it almost looked strange to see him smile like that but his blue eyes were genuine and though the tattoos that covered his left arm made him look like a badass, his grip on my hand had been gentle.

"Can you talk?" he asked, chuckling lightly as he leaned closer to me, inspecting me like a bug under a microscope.

"I just came to get my sister," I mumbled, shaking my head and looking down at Paige who looked to be sleeping deeply, curled up on the couch.

I shifted towards her, attempting to wedge my shoulders underneath her arm when suddenly, she was gone.

"Where to?" Dan asked, holding Paige easily in his arms, looking like he was carrying nothing more than a feather.

I blinked. "My car," I said quietly, nodding my head towards the stairs before looking away, following behind him when he began to move.

"What's with you?" Grayson asked suddenly, walking next to me up the stairs.

I shot him a questioning look, not sure what he meant.

"You're acting weird," he said, his eyes swinging forward as we neared the top of the stairs, a muscle in his jaw ticking. "Like you're scared or something. Is it Dan?"

"No," I mumbled, following Dan through the house, stepping over empty cups and avoided beer bottles that were scattered over the floor.

"Maybe you like him, then?" he asked, cutting a sly look in my direction. "I didn't really picture him as your type but I might be able to set something up if he's interested."

I gritted my teeth. "I don't like him."

"No?" Grayson asked as we walked through the door heading across the lawn towards my car. "Then how come you can barely string two words together in front of him but you have no problem yelling at me?"

"I——" I broke off, shaking my head. How did I explain it to him when I couldn't even explain it to myself? It was weird the way I went off on Grayson. I so rarely lost control like that but with him…I just couldn't seem to keep it in check.

"I see how it is," he said, his voice filled with disgust. "I'm just a lowlife piece of scum, right?" he snarled and I flinched, remembering how I'd called him that the first time we'd ever met.

"No," I said firmly, watching as Dan loaded Paige into the backseat of my car. Taking a deep breath, I faced Grayson, straightening my spine and preparing to do what I'd resolved to do the day before. Apologize. "I shouldn't have said that. I didn't mean it," I said, keeping my tone and expression neutral. "Also, you were right about the other night. I should've thanked you but I…" I trailed off, frowning slightly before I shook my head. "I was just having a bad night. Please forget about it." I paused, expecting him to say something, to rub it in my face but he just stayed silent, his eyes unreadable and that muscle in his jaw still ticking. "I'm sorry I was rude," I said with finality, giving a little nod of my head before turning my back on him, thanking Dan and rounding my car.

"Nell!" Craig said, running up to me just as I opened my car door. "You okay?" he said, his voice hushed as he leaned closer to me, gripping my elbow and casting a suspicious glance towards the other two guys.

"I'm fine," I said, trying to stretch my lips into a semblance of a smile but I was exhausted and run down. The terror of his phone call was still giving me chills even though Paige seemed okay now, I couldn't erase the image of her, pale and limp, her limbs slack and lifeless as she lay there with my pill bottle in her pocket. "I just…want to go home."

He bent his knees slightly, bringing our faces to the same level, his familiar blue eyes locking with mine as he nodded. "I'm sorry, Nell."

"Me too," I whispered, my throat clogging as I gestured to where I could see his vehicle, seeing Brian inside. "Thanks for calling."

My eyes widened when suddenly, Craig's arms were wrapped around me and he was giving me a tight squeeze. I stood stiffly in the short embrace, forgetting to breathe. I blinked up at him when he backed up, his eyes nowhere near mine. "I'll see you at school," he mumbled, turning his back on me and walking away.

"Yeah," I said, my voice so quiet that I could barely hear it. Had Craig Jensen just hugged me? I mean, sure we were kind of friends in the sense that we both looked after someone who shouldn't need looking after but...

We didn't hug.

Feeling a little shell shocked, I collapsed into my car, quickly shutting it behind me.

I sat inside and let out a long breath, shaking off my shock and glancing in the back seat at Paige. She was sleeping soundly, her chest rising and falling regularly. I faced forward again, feeling a little better because even though my sister was passed out, drunk and high on my drugs, at least she was alive and as an added bonus, I'd straightened things out with Grayson West. Now we could go back to ignoring each other.

I started my car and put it into drive, shoving the pill bottle I was still holding into a cup holder before glancing towards the two boys one more time. For a moment, I was caught by Grayson's expression. Where I'd expected to see cool indifference, instead I saw...anger. Had I said something wrong? Did I unconsciously insult him again?

With a sigh, I pulled away from the curb, resolving not to think about it. He was probably angry about something else. There could be a million other things that had nothing to do with me.

Yeah, that was probably it. As far as I was concerned, Grayson West and I had no reason to ever talk to each other again.

This was good.

This was perfect.

Chapter 4

Nell's POV

I stopped the car in our driveway and shut off the engine. For a long moment, I sat there and listened to Paige's soft snores, relief and anger creating a strange cocktail in my gut.

My eyes slid to the cup-holder next to me and I slowly reached out to pick up the pill bottle sitting there.

Klonopin.

Did she even get it? Did she even understand what she was taking?

She could've died.

"Tell me you didn't pick me up," Paige groaned from the backseat.

My hand tightened around the pill bottle. "I did."

"Oh god," she grumbled. I watched in the mirror as she sat up and scratched her forehead with fingernails painted purple. "Did people see you?"

"Yes."

"Great. And I was doing so good at pretending I didn't know you." She shifted towards the door and pushed it open, sliding out to stand unsteadily on the interlocking stones of our driveway.

Rage pulsed under my skin, making my vision go a little hazy as I reached out to open my own door.

Her steps were slow so it wasn't hard to catch up to her.

"How much did you take?" I asked, my voice quiet and shaky as I thrust the pill bottle under her nose and gripped her forearm, forcing her to stop just in front of the door.

"Just a couple," she said, rolling her eyes, her lips spreading into a mocking grin. "Let me go, spaz."

"Do even know what this is?" I hissed, tightening my grip on her arm and pulling her closer to me, my anger reaching a boiling point as she tried to brush me off.

She shrugged. "Something that's supposed to help you loosen up would be my guess." Her eyes seemed clear for a second as they locked on mine, a knowing glow in their depths. "Which, now that I mention it, is a bit suspicious. You're just as uptight as ever, Nellie. You've got all these pretty little bottles lined up in your medicine cabinet. You can't tell me you take those meds and you're still this fucked up."

"This isn't about me," I snapped, letting her arm go to run a shaking hand through my hair. "You mixed Klonopin with alcohol, Paige. You could've di——"

"Don't be so dramatic," she said, waving her hand dismissively as she placed her other one on the door knob. "Besides, if I didn't take them, who would? What do you do, Nell? Flush them down the toilet?" She tilted her head back and laughed in my face. "I suppose I should've known. When you first came back at the end of the summer, you were a totally different person, a complete space case. But now you're back to your old spazzy ways." Her lips tilted up further as she leaned a bit closer to me, her hand on the doorknob helping her keep her balance. "All your pill bottles were alphabetized, Nell. Want to tell me how normal you are? Care to convince me that you're not insane?" She snorted, her eyes narrowing on me as my breath came in short pants, my hands fisted so hard at my sides that my nails were digging into my flesh. "Look at you. You're a fucking nut job. Why don't you just give up? Mom and Dad are never going to take you seriously, so why don't you just quit trying and go back to the loony bin where you belong."

Everything inside of me went still as I stared at my younger sister, my hand slowly falling away from her forearm.

I squinted at her face, searching for a sign that she hadn't meant it, that she regretted those words but her eyes were cold, anger and hate shining from their blue depths.

She really hates me.

I felt like a part of me was dying as I looked at the girl in front of me for what felt like the first time. This wasn't the same Paige I'd sat outside with, watching the stars. This wasn't the Paige who would hug me when I was sad.

No. This Paige was different.

"You think I belong in an institution."

Her lips stretched into a cold smile. "Yes."

That one word sent a wave of despair through me, threatening to buckle my knees with its force. "You really think I'm crazy, don't you?" I asked in a weak voice, already knowing the answer.

She rolled her eyes, not bothering with an answer as she turned away from me and opened the door.

I don't know how long I stood there in the open doorway, watching as my sister walked away from me, her words still ringing in my head.

Go back to the loony bin where you belong.

My fingers started to ache from keeping my hands fisted for so long. My jaw was clenched so hard that I was afraid I'd chip a tooth.

Get a grip, Nell. You already knew how she felt.

I sucked in a deep breath through my nose, trying to calm the rage and hurt thundering through my veins. She didn't understand. How could I make her understand?

I lifted the pill bottle in my hand, shaking it slightly to see the contents. Funny how I could spend the past few months running away from these stupid pills while Paige went out of her way to take them. I hated these pills. I hated the way they made me feel, I hated the person they turned me into.

But most of all, I hated the way they were prescribed.

Each time it had been the same. A therapist would ask me a few questions and whether I answered honestly or not, they'd prescribe me something, something that would numb me, calm me, correct me, fucking fix me.

For a while, I thought that if I just went along with it, if I just took the pills like a good little girl, everything would change. Like those small little white tablets would make my parents look at me as something other than an embarrassment.

God, I was stupid.

Straightening my shoulders, I walked into the house silently, closing and locking the door behind me. The pill bottle felt heavy in my hand as I tightened my fingers around it, wishing I could just flush the contents down the toilet.

But then Eleanor would notice and I'd lose everything.

She was just waiting for the opportunity to send me away. All she needed was an excuse and doing something like that...

Bye, bye, Nell.

I walked up the stairs quickly, going straight through my room and into the small bathroom attached. My hands shook as I opened the medicine cabinet, revealing my alphabetized pill bottles within. There were about a dozen of them, some stronger than others. None of them were meant to be mixed with alcohol.

My heart thundered as I thought about what could've happened to Paige. I gritted my teeth as I stared at those bottles, hating them so strongly that my fingers twitched with the need to open each bottle and dump the contents.

If I did that, it would all be over.

There'd be no pretending anymore. College would be out the window. They'd pull me from school, send me to an institution and no matter how hard I tried, no one would ever look at me as anything close to normal ever again.

Least of all, my family.

I wanted to not care. I wanted to forget about the Nell I was always trying to be, to forget about that pervasive need to do everything right, to please them and just throw out those fucking pills.

Instead, with a shaking hand, I closed the medicine cabinet, leaving my alphabetized pills inside, untouched.

"Well done, Nell," Mr. Ford said, placing my marked paper on the desk in front of me.

"Thank you," I said quietly, my lips stretching into a polite smile as I watched him move on to the next student.

I looked down at my paper and my heart tripped uncomfortably in my chest, lodging into my throat.

An A minus.

He'd given me an A minus?

Gritting my teeth, I flipped through the paper, crinkling the pages as I searched for any red marks, needing to understand why the hell it didn't deserve an A.

Nothing. There was nothing.

How could he do that and offer no explanation? How could he dock me marks without telling me what I needed to do to improve?

A bitter taste filled my mouth as my breathing started to come a little faster, wheezing in and out of my lungs.

The girl in the desk beside me was looking at me. I could feel her eyes on my skin, judging me, probably thinking I was nuts.

Relax, Nell.

I tried to suck in a deeper breath, tried to act somewhat normal but I couldn't shake the panic that was building inside of me.

Reaching out, I compulsively straightened my pens, my eyes darting to the left and connecting with the girl's sitting next to me. Her brows were raised and her lips were quirked in a slight, mocking grin that made me grind my teeth.

The bell rang. "Okay folks, I'll see you Wednesday," Mr. Ford said as students hastily gathered their things and stood from their chairs.

Ignoring the whispers from the girl beside me and her friends, I stood too and walked towards Mr. Ford's desk.

"Excuse me, Mr. Ford?" I said, my voice coming out squeaky and timid. I flinched at the sound of it and I think I saw pity in my teacher's eyes as they connected with mine.

"What can I do for you, Nell?"

I swallowed hard and bit my lip, a part of me knowing I was being ridiculous but another part of me just couldn't keep her mouth shut. "I was wondering about my grade. Why is it an A minus? What did I do wrong?"

"That's the highest grade in the class, Nell. You should be proud of your work."

My stomach dropped and I wanted to laugh. "But it could've been better, right? Can you explain how?"

"It was a challenging paper to write. I just felt that it didn't quite deserve a full A."

God, why wasn't he giving me a straight answer? I wanted to slam my hands onto the desk in frustration. I wanted to lean in and intimidate him into telling me why.

He was right. It had been a challenging paper to write. I'd worked my ass off making sure it was perfect and this was how he rewarded me? An A minus?

"I felt like it was worth an A," I blurted, wanting to slap a hand over my mouth as soon as the words were out. What was I doing? Arguing with a teacher?

This wasn't me. I didn't argue with teachers. I didn't argue with anyone.

Just Grayson West.

Mr. Ford's eyes narrowed slightly on me. "I guess that's why I'm the teacher, and you're the student."

"But if you'd just explain——"

"I gave the grade the paper deserved. Just put a little more thought into your arguments next time and I'm sure you'll get an A. Now, it's lunch time and I'm starving so please, head to the cafeteria, Miss Watson."

"More thought?" I snapped, leaning towards him further, my fingers digging into the books I was carrying. I wanted to tilt my head back and laugh at the ridiculous notion. I'd researched that paper until my eyes crossed. I'd started working on it the day it was assigned and never once forgot about it until I handed it in.

He wanted me to put more thought into it?

What a fucking joke.

"Nell?"

I blinked, realizing Mr. Ford was looking at me with alarm, his gaze focused on where one of my hands had landed on his desk. I was leaning on it, glaring down at him as I crushed a few scattered papers beneath my palm.

With a slight gasp, I pulled my hand back, stumbling a little in my haste to retreat. "S-sorry," I mumbled, turning my back and practically running from the classroom, ignoring Mr. Ford as he called out to me several times.

"Oh my god," I whispered, my breath hissing in and out of my lungs, burning my throat. Shame and embarrassment wound through me, making bile rise in my throat. What was wrong with me? I'd nearly lost it in there. I'd seriously come close to shouting at him for not giving me an A.

Way to convince everyone that you're not a lunatic, Nell.

I winced as I slammed my palm into the door to the ladies bathroom, my heart thundering in my chest as I pushed into a stall and sat on the toilet, leaning my head on my hands and working on breathing normally as my brain worked furiously to make sense of the situation.

I felt like I was losing it. I felt like everything Paige had said to me that night had wormed its way into my skull and stuck there like a parasite. She thought I was insane, she thought I belonged in an institution.

Why don't you just give up?

I groaned and rubbed my temples, my panic finally starting to recede slightly even as a thought pressed at my brain, demanding attention.

I couldn't keep going like this.

I felt like I was standing on the edge of a cliff, that all it would take was one more little push and I'd be falling.

I was starting to think that it wouldn't even need to be a hard push. Maybe just a light breeze would knock me over at this point.

The coil inside of my chest was wound so tightly that it was at breaking point and if I didn't find some way to loosen it soon, it would snap and take me with it.

Only...

I didn't know how to do it. I didn't know how to let off steam, how to release the tension that was always part of me unless...

Unless I took the drugs the doctors were prescribing me.

They took the tension away but they took everything else too. I hated the numb feeling they gave me, like I was a bystander in my own life, watching as I went through the motions. I didn't want to go back to that.

With a sigh, I ran my hands over my hair, checking for any strays and tucking them into my bun. Finally feeling like I could at least face the rest of the day, I stood and exited the bathroom, walking around the hallways in a daze. My eyes slid over the other students just as their eyes slid over me. I was disconnected, apart, constantly focused on the pressure that was piling on my shoulders.

It used to be different. I used to have Paige. She was always my safe haven, my escape.

Now she hated me.

I rounded a corner and I nearly crashed into Grayson West as he rounded the same corner from the other direction.

My hand jutted out and landed on his chest to keep my balance as his hand shot out and gripped my shoulder, his big hand immediately spreading warmth down my arm.

I opened my mouth to apologize, to mumble something inane before walking away but nothing happened. Instead, we stood there, our eyes locked on each other, my hand still on his chest and his still on my shoulder as if frozen in that position.

"Gray?"

I blinked at the feminine voice, my gaze shifting to over his shoulder where I could see a beautiful redheaded girl walking towards us, her lips tilted into a familiar, mocking grin as her eyes landed on me.

"What are you doing?" she asked, her gaze sliding from me to Grayson but he didn't move. His head shifted but he was looking down, his eyes focused on my arm and then my hand where it rested on his chest. His lips tilted into a half smile and I frowned, trying to figure out what he thought was funny when I realized my fingers had curled slightly and my hand was no longer just resting on his chest, it was actually gripping the material of his t-shirt like I had no intention of letting go.

As soon as the thought crossed my mind, I jerked away from him, shoving my offending hand into my pocket as I muttered a breathless, "Sorry," and ducked under his arm, my face flaming with embarrassment as I practically sprinted away from him, feeling his eyes on my back the entire time until I turned down a different hallway, not even caring where I was going as long as I was out of his line of sight.

"Idiot," I mumbled, shaking my head at my own actions, pulling my hand out of my pocket to flex my fingers. What had I been thinking? He was probably still laughing at me, mocking the crazy chick who'd stared at him and clung to his t-shirt like a freak while his girlfriend watched.

I winced. I thought I was over making a fool of myself in front of Grayson West.

Guess not.

The rest of the day was a blur. My mind wouldn't focus. I was constantly thinking about that A minus and my near freak out, worrying that I was losing it for real this time.

It was a relief when the day was over and for the first time since I got fired, I thought it might be a blessing that I didn't have to go to work after school.

Maybe I'd go for a drive somewhere, pretend I never had to come back, that I could just drive as far as my car could take me and then start over again.

Only, when I put the key in the ignition and turned, my car made a sad little sound and died.

I blinked at the steering wheel, trying again but this time there was no sound at all.

My lips stretched and hysterical laughter burned its way up my throat, forcing its way out of my mouth until I couldn't hold it in anymore. I tilted my head back, and let it out, giving in.

So, this was as far as my car would take me, huh?

There goes my escape plan.

Still chuckling lightly, I popped the hood, hoping the battery was just disconnected or something. I could probably handle that.

I got out of my car and propped the hood up, frowning down at the foreign contents in front of me. All necessary wires seemed to be connected to the battery and as far as I could tell, nothing was on fire.

In my expert opinion, the vehicle should've been running smoothly.

"Hey, Nell!"

I jumped slightly at the sound of Paige's voice, turning on my heel to look towards her. She was sitting in the passenger side of Brian's car, her lips spread into a wide grin. "Car troubles?"

I gritted my teeth, not even bothering to respond.

She just laughed and gave me the middle finger as Brian peeled out of the parking lot, leaving a cloud of dust in his wake.

"Nice," I muttered, waving my hand in front of my face, choking on the dust cloud his car had kicked up.

I gathered my things from inside of the car, deciding that I'd leave it there until I could figure something else out. I didn't really have the money to get it fixed right now but maybe if I googled "how to fix my crappy car" I'd find some inspiration.

I was reaching for my bag when the sound of a loud engine roared closer to me before cutting off. I blinked a couple of times, wondering if I was hearing things or if the engine had really cut off directly behind me.

"I think it's time to get a new car, Cupcake."

I winced at the sound of his voice saying that stupid nickname again. "Don't call me that," I ground out, a part of me thinking that the anger swirling inside of me was misplaced, that the past few days were just coming to a peak and Grayson happened to be standing behind me, calling me Cupcake.

"Seriously, this thing is a piece of junk."

My hand, still outstretched towards my bag, fisted and I pulled back to face him, spinning on my heel until our eyes met. "What do you want, Grayson?" I snapped, forgetting that I was keeping it cool when it came to him.

He made a sound of frustration and crossed his arms over his chest, leaning against his bike in a deceptively casual pose. "Why do you always do that, Cupcake? Why are you automatically on the defensive when I talk to you?"

I snorted. "Maybe it's because you always call me that stupid nickname!" I half shouted, my breath coming a little faster as I took a step towards him.

"It's just a nickname, Nell. Maybe I'm just trying to be friendly."

I rolled my eyes. "That seems highly unlikely."

"Why?" he snapped, uncrossing his arms and closing the distance between us in two long, angry strides. "You don't think I can be friendly?"

"Why would you bother, Grayson? We're not friends. We're never going to be friends, so whether my car is a piece of shit or not, it's none of your business."

His back bowed a little and his face came so close to mine that I could feel his breath across my lips. His eyes were pitch black now, fury clear in their depths as he glared at me. "Trust me, Cupcake, I know we're not friends. It's pretty fucking obvious by the disgusted look on your face when you see me and the way you can hardly speak to me without getting that snotty tone in your voice. Even if I didn't notice any of that, I'd just have to take one look at the fucking mansion you live in and I'd know for sure that we're never going to be anything close to best buds."

"It has nothing to do with that," I hissed, pushing on his chest but he wasn't budging.

"Oh yeah? Could've fooled me, Nell. You have no problem hugging Mr. Trust Fund from the party, yet you can barely look in my direction without getting nauseous."

I made a sound of frustration in the back of my throat and pushed harder against his chest but the guy was solid. "You could be a millionaire and I still wouldn't be able to have a civil conversation with you, Grayson. We don't get along. That's all there is to it, so please just leave me alone so I can figure out how to deal with my crappy car without having to worry about yelling at you at the same time!"

His jaw clenched and his eyes flashed with anger as we stood there, chest to chest, neither of us breathing very steadily. "Fine," he growled after what felt like an eternity.

Finally, he took a step back, his jaw still tight and his shoulders stiff as he turned his back on me, striding towards his bike.

I turned back towards my car, residual anger making my hands shake as I reached into my car to grab my stuff, intent on walking home and mentally bashing Grayson West over the head as many times as I could with various imaginary objects.

I slung the strap of my bag over my shoulder and slammed the car door shut, inwardly wincing as I did so, worried that the whole thing might just crumble from the force. I didn't look in Grayson's direction even though I was curious. He hadn't started his bike yet and he'd had plenty of time to be on his merry way.

What was the hold up?

Why do I even care?

I shook my head, facing the sidewalk with determination, deciding that I didn't care, that it didn't matter to me one little bit why he wasn't jetting it away from there, pushing his bike as fast as it could possibly go just to get away from a psycho like me.

Nope, doesn't matter.

"Cupcake?"

My feet stopped immediately at the sound of his voice, my hands clenching into fists because he'd used that stupid nickname, but like a moth inexorably drawn to the flame, I turned to face him with a brow raised in question.

He still looked pissed off, his jaw still set at a harsh slant, his eyes still darker than usual. As I watched, he reached up to brush a hand through his too-long hair, his forehead wrinkling as he looked over at me.

"Do you need a ride?"

I blinked slowly, wondering if I'd heard him right. Hadn't we just been fighting five seconds ago? What in that whole conversation translated to him offering me a ride anywhere?

Besides, I'd been on that bike once before and I'd been drunk. There was no way I'd be getting on that thing again, sober and perfectly able to make logical decisions.

I opened my mouth, the refusal poised on my lips, set in stone in my head, forming on my tongue.

"Okay."

What?

What the fuck did I just say?

Had I just agreed, in a sober state, to get on Grayson West's motorcycle?

Not possible.

But judging by the way he was walking towards me with one corner of his mouth kind of quirked and a spare helmet in his hand, it suddenly seemed likely.

"Hop on, Cupcake," he said as he handed me the helmet, his smile widening slightly as I hesitated, my hands gripping the strap of my bag tightly, trying to figure out how to take it back.

My eyes latched onto his and it was the dare I saw in their depths that did me in. He didn't think I'd do it and for whatever reason, that bothered me. So, with more confidence than I felt, I reached out and grabbed the helmet, tilting my chin into the air as I pulled it from his hands.

I think his smile became smug as he turned away from me and got on the bike, but his features were blank when he jerked his head towards the space behind him, indicating that I should get on now.

I'm an idiot, I thought as I pulled the helmet on my head, making sure all the straps were tightened until I felt like I couldn't breathe.

"Oh my god," I whispered, throwing a leg over the death trap, my heart skittering around inside of my rib cage wildly as I settled onto the seat, compulsively tightening the straps on my bag, making sure it was secure on my back. "Why did I agree to this?" I mumbled.

Grayson's shoulders shook slightly and I could've sworn he was laughing at me but then he started the bike up and the roar of the engine drowned everything else out. Terror swept through me and my hands latched onto the seat below me, my fingers digging into the metal and fabric until I thought I might break the skin.

"C'mon, Cupcake, don't be shy," he said, reaching back and gripping my wrists, pulling my arms around his waist before letting go.

Before I had the chance to respond, we were moving and once we were moving, there was no way I was changing my position unless it was to hold on tighter.

It was worse than I remembered.

I think I'd been imagining a sense of freedom, of weightlessness from the first time but that feeling was gone now. All that was left was terror. We flew through neighbourhoods, seeming to pick up speed around corners as we tilted dangerously. I felt like my knees were going to scrape against the ground every time we turned but logically, I knew they were nowhere near the pavement. I wanted to shout at Grayson to slow down but when I managed to spot the speedometer, I saw that we were actually going below the speed limit.

I bit my tongue and closed my eyes after that, my arms tightening further around him without thought.

And then something changed.

I started to relax and my brain kind of…flicked off. It was strange but for a few moments, I felt like we weren't even touching the ground, like the world around us didn't exist and the only thing that mattered was that we kept moving forward.

I frowned when we turned a corner and slowed down before coming to a stop. It was on the tip of my tongue to tell him to just keep driving and I think I sat there for a long time with my arms wrapped around him and my eyes closed, the bike unmoving beneath us.

"I need to get off, Cupcake," he said, his voice a little quieter, a little gruffer than usual.

I blinked my eyes open, releasing him immediately and shifting back a little on the seat. "Where are we?" I asked when I managed to take in the scene in front of me. We definitely weren't at my parent's house.

"Just a quick pit stop. I have to pick up my paycheque."

I quirked a brow, climbing off the bike quickly, my knees feeling a bit wobbly from the sense of gravity pushing down on me once more.

"You work here?" I asked, looking around at the large, fenced in area. There were stacks of wood all over the place, some of them bigger than others. The smell of fresh cut trees invaded my senses and I found myself taking deep breaths through my nose, enjoying the scent.

"Yeah," he said simply, walking ahead of me towards the large warehouse in the centre of the complex.

I stood by the bike awkwardly, shifting my weight from foot to foot, not sure if I should follow him or not.

"You coming?" he asked after a moment, pausing to glance over his shoulder at me, his expression blank and his shoulders a bit stiff.

I don't know why I did it. I should've just stayed there and waited for him but my head was nodding and my feet were carrying me towards him before I really had a chance to think about it.

I caught up to him and we walked together into the building. I kept glancing over at him, feeling weird about the way we were moving, side by side, almost like we were...hanging out.

I thought about Paige and what she might say if she knew I'd willingly taken a ride on the back of Grayson West's motorcycle.

She'd probably call me crazy.

Nothing new with that.

Oddly, a smile threatened the stretch my lips at the thought. At least this time, her accusations would be founded.

"West," an older man said, giving Grayson a warm smile as he approached us from a door leading to the back of the warehouse. "Come to get your paycheque?" he asked, his eyes slipping over to me in question. "Who's this?"

"This is Cupcake," he said with a smirk, making my spine stiffen. "We go to school together," Wes filled in.

"My name," I snapped, glaring over at Grayson, "is Nell," I finished, giving a small, polite smile to the older man.

He wiped his hands on a dirty handkerchief before reaching over to shake my hand. "Nice to meet you, Nell, I'm Jim," he said with a smile that softened his features and automatically made me want to smile back.

"Nice to meet you," I said, feeling at ease around him for some reason. Maybe it was because he wasn't looking at me with that glint of recognition in his eyes that came with the knowledge that I wasn't 'all there' in the head.

"Nice to meet you…t-too," I stuttered when suddenly Jim's hand tightened on mine and that recognition I was pleased to not see in his eyes began to shimmer across their blue depths.

"Are you Nell Watson?" he asked and I hastily pulled my hand away from his, looking down at the sawdust covered floor.

"Yes," I said softly, my heart starting to beat more rapidly. I glanced over my shoulder, eager for an escape. Why had I come in here?

"I know your dad," he said, something in his voice telling me that he wasn't entirely happy about that.

"Don't worry, I'm nothing like him."

I blinked, my wide eyes locking on Jim's for a second as my words registered. What did I just say?

"I mean..I-I——"

Jim tilted his head back and gave a long, hearty laugh, cutting off my attempts at an excuse. "I'm happy to hear that, Nell. Your dad and I don't exactly see eye to eye."

I nodded and gave him a stiff smile, worried that if I opened my mouth, something unwanted would escape my lips again. What was going on with me today? First, I'd argued with Mr. Ford, then I'd agreed to get a ride from Grayson and now I was badmouthing my father to a total stranger?

I needed to get myself under control.

Still chuckling lightly, Jim shifted a few papers on the reception desk, looking for the right one before picking up an envelope and handing it to Grayson. "You going to be on time tomorrow, West?"

"We'll see," Grayson said with a slow smile and a hint of laughter in his voice.

"Next time you're late, I'm docking your pay."

Grayson rolled his eyes. "I'll believe it when I see it, old man."

"I'm serious this time," Jim said in a stern voice but his eyes were twinkling and I could see the affection he had for Grayson written all over his face.

I couldn't believe it, Grayson West actually got along with his boss?

What really surprised me was that he had a boss. Considering his reputation as a badass, shouldn't he be a drug dealer or something?

Instead he worked...in a lumber yard?

It just didn't add up.

"Of course you are, Jim. Of course you are," Grayson said, flashing a grin at Jim and for a second, I couldn't tear my eyes away from him. His face changed when he smiled. That hardness that seemed to always be present vanished and his dark eyes seemed to become a couple shades lighter, the golds and browns catching the light.

He waved goodbye to his boss and turned towards me, his eyes catching on mine and his smile vanished as his brow furrowed. "What's with you?" he asked, his tone no longer quite as open and friendly as it had been with Jim.

"Nothing," I mumbled, shaking my head and focusing on the ground.

"Okay," he said slowly, letting out a breath. "Let's get out of here."

I nodded and followed him out of the door, feeling a strange energy shift through me at the thought of climbing back onto that bike again. I was still scared of it, still convinced that I'd probably die if we dared to turn a corner but at the same time, I was drawn to it, to that feeling I'd briefly captured when I'd closed my eyes, when I'd just…let go.

It wasn't really a sensation I was familiar with.

I watched as Grayson put his helmet on and mounted the bike, starting it up smoothly, his hands moving through the steps as if it were second nature to him.

"You coming?" he asked, pushing the visor back from his helmet so he could raise a brow in my direction.

I nodded but my feet were frozen in place, my eyes drifting over the complicated buttons and dials on the bike. "Is it hard to drive one of those?" I asked, raising my voice to be heard over the noise of the machine.

His other brow lifted to join the first and for a long moment, he didn't say anything, just stared at me as if I was a breed of animal he'd never seen before. "Why? You want to learn, Cupcake?"

I took a half step back and shook my head hard. "No!" I half shouted, my heart rate increasing in panic at the very thought of being the one in control of such a dangerous machine.

"You sure?" he said, his tone slightly mocking as he cut the engine and swung his leg back over the bike, dismounting and gesturing for me to take the front seat.

"What are you doing?" I asked, my wide eyes swinging from him to the bike and back again as I took a step away from him.

"Giving you your first lesson, Cupcake," he said, advancing towards me with a smug smile on his lips.

"No thanks," I said, holding my hands out in front of me to ward him off. "I can't even hold a job at a coffee shop. What makes you think I'd be able to drive one of those things?" I said, pointing an accusatory finger at the bike.

"You got fired?" Grayson said, his expression registering total shock. "Are you serious?"

I shrugged, looking at a point over his shoulder as embarrassment made my cheeks heat.

"What did they fire you for? Being too perfect?"

"I'm not perfect," I snapped, my eyes narrowing as I took a step towards him, anger outweighing my fear for the moment.

"Oh come on, Nell, I've been going to the same school as you for four years now. Aside from one night with a bottle of champagne, I've yet to see you screw anything up," he said, pulling his helmet off his head.

"Don't act like you know everything about me. You didn't even know who I was until the night of that party where you pretended to own the car blocking me in," I snapped, anger making my hands clench into fists at my sides.

He just shrugged, his eyes shifting to the side as he stood up again. "Why is this turning into a fight again? You seemed interested so I offered to teach you how to ride a bike. Somehow, that makes me a bad person but I guess I shouldn't be surprised when it comes to you."

I frowned and shook my head, wishing I could just shut my mouth around him for once. "I was just curious, Grayson. I just...wanted to know how it works. I could never actually drive something like that."

"How will you know unless you try?" he asked, his voice a bit softer than it had been, his dark eyes daring me to do it even as they shone with the knowledge that I wouldn't.

For a long moment, I simply stared at this guy I barely knew who seemed to get a kick out of pissing me off and who seemed to have a special talent for pushing my buttons.

I wanted to say no, to tell him that it really didn't matter if I ever learned how to ride a bike because after today, I'd likely never go on one again.

I really wanted to ignore him and walk away from there.

Instead, I grabbed my helmet and, with a deep, fortifying breath, asked, "Okay, where do I start?"

He flashed a quick smile before moving to give me space to climb on the bike. "Alright," he said, once I was settled and staring down at the complicated looking controls in front of me. I felt the bike dip when he sat behind me and my heart froze in my chest when his arms shifted around me, reaching forward to rest on the handles, effectively caging me in. "First thing is to kick the stand," he said, his voice way too close to my ear. God, did he have to be plastered all over me?

"Maybe it would be better if you weren't on the bike when you taught me," I said, my voice sounding strangled and weird.

"You're kidding, right? You want me to stand off to the side while you try to drive my motorcycle for the first time? Not going to happen, Cupcake." I gritted my teeth and tried to shift forward a bit so we weren't quite as pressed together as we had been. "Am I making you uncomfortable, Nell?" he asked huskily.

"Not at all," I lied, willing my heart rate to slow down a little.

He chuckled lightly and pushed us forward, kicking the stand at the same time until the only thing keeping us from tipping over was our feet on the ground.

"Turn the key in the ignition," he said, pointing me in the right direction. I nodded and did as I was told, watching as the dials shifted and lights came on. "See this light?" he said, pointing at a green light on the dash. I nodded. "It means it's in neutral. You should be in neutral when you start. Now, press this button." I swallowed hard and pressed the starter, making the bike roar to life.

My lips spread into an unconscious grin that I squashed quickly. Was I seriously enjoying this?

Impossible.

"Okay, down here is the shifter," he said and I looked down where he was pointing, listening as he taught me how to change gears, absorbing the information and asking questions when I was unsure. It was weird to think it, but Grayson West was actually a patient teacher. He didn't lose his temper when I asked a bunch of questions about the clutch and how much to release it and how will I know when I'm actually in first gear. He just answered me calmly, walking me through the steps without being condescending.

"Ready to move?" he asked after taking me through the process of getting into first a few times.

I nodded, swallowing nervously as excitement skittered across my skin.

"Hold the clutch." I did, a shiver rippling over my skin at the feel of his hand over mine, guiding me on how much pressure to put on the clutch. "Now, give it some gas," he said, twisting the throttle with me until we moved forward slightly and slowly, he released the clutch until we moved into first gear.

I laughed out loud as I guided the bike around the parking lot, glad that it was mostly empty.

"Ready for second gear?" he shouted and I nodded, grinning from ear to ear.

Okay, so maybe I was enjoying this. Sue me.

"Give a little more gas," he said, still guiding my hands, pressing the clutch down with me as we started to move faster.

The shift into second was even smoother than the shift into first and I laughed again as we circled the parking lot at a faster pace.

"You good?" he asked, pulling his hands slightly away from mine and I nodded, eager to be driving the bike without his help even if it was just for a second. He let go of the handles completely and I felt a brief moment of elation before he settled his hands on my hips and I felt my stomach drop.

"Steady," he said, his voice pulling me back, reminding me that I was still driving a motorcycle, that I didn't have time to worry about the way his hands felt on me, the way it was almost...intimate.

The thought of any intimacy between the two of us made me give a short laugh and had my brain snapping back to the present. What a joke. A guy like Grayson would never be interested in a girl like me. He was just...being nice for some inexplicable reason. Maybe it was his idea of giving to charity.

Whatever it was, I didn't care. I rode the bike around the parking lot a few more times, unable to wipe the grin off my face the entire ride.

When we finally came to a stop and Grayson walked me through the steps of turning the bike off, I was still smiling. The bike shifted when he got off and I looked over at him, grinning like a fool as I took off my helmet, exhilaration coursing through my veins. "That was incredible," I said, barely recognizing my own voice as it shook with excitement.

"You liked it, huh?" he said, taking off his helmet to stare down at me, an odd expression on his face, like he was seeing me for the first time.

I nodded and moved to stand so he could take his place at the front of the bike once more. "I would die to see the expression on my parent's faces if they knew I'd done that," I said, my body still humming with excitement.

"What, you don't think they'd approve?" Grayson asked with a mock look of disbelief on his face.

"Not a chance," I said with a laugh, loving that they'd be pissed at me, but loving even more that they would never in a million years think I'd drive a motorcycle without their permission.

I was always the dependable one, always the one who would never break the rules. I was too desperate for their approval, too focused on being the perfect daughter to even think to step out of line.

And before the Johnston's party, they would've been right.

But now…

What was the point in working so hard for approval that was never going to come?

"I can't believe I drove a motorcycle," I said, my grin still not fading as I looked up at Grayson in wonder.

"I'm pretty surprised myself," he said, his voice quiet now, a bit gruff as he stared down at me with questions in his eyes. "I can't figure you out, Nell Watson."

I shrugged, my grin fading as I looked at the ground, kicking a stray rock as my spine stiffened. "What's to figure out," I mumbled.

"What's the deal with you and your parents? Why are you so happy to do something they wouldn't like?"

"Cause I never do," I said softly, a half smile stretching my lips as I looked up at him, ignoring the voice in my head that was telling me to shut up. "It's a nice change of pace." I let out a slow breath and closed my eyes for a second, thinking about the coil in my chest and the panic that rose in my throat every time something wasn't perfect. "Maybe I should just stop trying to impress them."

"We could go rob a liquor store, if you want."

My eyes shot open to see that he was grinning at me and I couldn't seem to stop the smile from spreading across my own lips. What was going on here? When had we gone from snapping at each other to smiling?

"I think I'll pass on the felonies for today," I said.

"Well, let me know if you change your mind," he said, grabbing my helmet and plopping it on my head. "C'mon Cupcake, let's get out of here."

This time when I got on the bike, I didn't even hesitate to wrap my arms around his waist, knowing he'd probably force me to put them there, anyway.

I closed my eyes again, letting myself forget where I was, for once, not caring about the world around me as I drank in the sensation of being on a motorcycle.

Too soon, we came to a stop and I opened my eyes, seeing that we were parked at the end of my block.

"I think your mom just pulled into the driveway, Cupcake. Maybe I should just let you off here."

I nodded my head, reaching up to pull off my helmet but suddenly, I stopped. Why should he drop me off a block away? What did it matter if she saw me drive up on a motorcycle? Wasn't I supposed to not care?

"It's okay," I heard myself say, my ears ringing slightly at the thought of what I was about to do.

"What?" Grayson asked, turning his body slightly as he lifted his visor, trying to look at me.

I leaned to the side so I could meet his gaze. "I mean, if it's okay with you, I think I might like it if you dropped me off at my house. Not here."

For a long beat, he just stared at me, his brows quirked, his expression blank. Then, a mischievous smile split his lips, his dark eyes dancing with amusement. "I could be cool with that."

Grayson's POV

I watched as her lips stretched into an answering smile, making something in my gut lurch. Who knew Nell Watson had such a great smile?

Her lips were full and slightly pouty and her teeth were straight and white and when she smiled, it was real. There was no artifice in her silver eyes and there was a dimple in her left cheek that had my fingers itching to trace the slight dip.

I blinked and gave my head a mental shake, telling myself to knock it off. This was Cupcake I was thinking about. The girl who organized her pencils and could hardly look at me without chewing my head off.

Only...

I couldn't seem to stop looking at her, to stop trying to get her to smile.

"Good," she said, that bewitching smile still on her lips, her bun, now loosened from its usual smooth hold, was hanging out of the bottom of her helmet, strands of her hair all over the place.

Good what? What were we talking about again?

Oh yeah, she wanted to put on a little show for her darling mother.

My grin widened as I laughed lightly and faced forward. "Hold on, Cupcake," I said, waiting until I felt her arms wrapping around my waist, ignoring the way my skin heated beneath my jacket wherever she touched me. Eyeing her mother down the street, I waited until she'd gotten a hold of all the bags she'd been unloading from her SUV and was heading towards the house before I revved the engine.

The tires skidded slightly as the bike shot forward as I slipped into second gear without a hitch. It took us barely a second to reach the driveway and I hit the brakes harder than I normally would, letting the tires slide across the pavement just enough to tick any parent off.

I nodded over at Mrs. Watson, noting the expensive brand names on the bags she was carrying, practically smelling money on her from here.

Nell slid off the bike and turned her back to her mother as she pulled the helmet off her head, making her already messy hair even more so. "Thanks for the ride," she said, her lips tilted into a half smile, one corner lifting a little higher than the other.

"Anytime," I said, shooting a look at her mother who was frozen in the exact place she'd been standing when I stopped. "I think she's pissed."

Nell's smile widened. "I know."

My eyes went a little unfocused for a second as she handed me the helmet. I reached out automatically to take it from her but lifted my other hand to grip her wrist and drag her a step closer to me. "You know what would piss her off even more?" I heard myself say, my heart beating a little faster as I felt her smooth skin beneath my callused hand.

"What?" she asked, her smile fading just a bit as she gave me a questioning look.

If I kissed you.

Wait, what?

Where the hell had that come from?

I blinked and focused on her face as she lifted a brow at me, waiting. "If you were driving," I said hastily, trying to pretend that the other thought had never crossed my mind.

She grinned. "Maybe next time," she said before turning her back on me and walking towards her mother.

I watched as she moved past Mrs. Watson, barely pausing to glance at her before she disappeared inside the house.

I sat there staring after her for a while, my brain stuck on that moment when those words had almost slipped out of my mouth. I needed to get my head on straight when it came to this girl.

Movement drew my eye and I shifted my gaze to her mother, watching as the woman made a shooing motion with her hand, her face a mask of fury and embarrassment.

I rolled my eyes and stuck the spare helmet back in its compartment, flipping the visor down on my own helmet before giving her a cheerful wave and revving the engine, burning out and leaving a black mark on the pavement before booking it away from Mrs. Watson and her confusing daughter.

A daughter who happened to have an amazing smile.

Chapter 5

Nell's POV

"What the hell was that?"

I forced myself to stop smiling as I turned towards my mother, my feet on the bottom step leading up to my room. "I got a ride home."

"With whom?" she snapped, fury written on every line of her face.

I shrugged, ignoring the way my heart was starting to beat faster, anxiety creeping up on me as I did what I never did. Faced off with my mother.

"He's just a guy from school."

Rage burned in her eyes and she dropped her shopping bags, closing the distance between us in two long strides.

My anxiety tripled as she looked at me like I was two feet tall and even though I was standing a step above her, I felt it.

"Don't you ever, ever embarrass me like that again, do you hear me, Penelope? People like that boy don't belong around here."

"You don't even know him," I said, my voice cracking slightly as my panic threatened to choke me. God, she shouldn't affect me like this anymore. Why did I still care so much?

"I don't need to know him, Nell. He's got trash written all over him."

I lurched back in disgust, hating her more than ever in that moment. "You're such a snob," I hissed, my voice perfectly clear for once, my disgust making my anxiety fade for a moment.

"How dare you call me a snob!" she shouted, her hand lashing out to wrap her fingers around my bicep. "It's hard enough to keep people from talking about your issues without having you riding around on the back of some loser's motorcycle. Is it your mission to drag this family down, Nell?"

The words felt like a slap to the face, making me flinch. "How can you say that?" I whispered, my hands fisting at my sides. Couldn't she see? Didn't she get it? This family was all I ever thought about. It was driving me nuts trying to hold it together, trying to toe the line but it was getting confusing. There were too many lines I couldn't cross, too many rules I needed to follow in order to pass inspection.

"Sylvia warned me about this."

My eyes snapped to hers as my heart stopped dead in my chest. "What?" I wheezed.

"She told me this is how it would start, that I needed to watch for the signs."

I shook my head, frowning down at her. "What signs? What are you talking about?"

"You're acting out, talking back, it's a symptom that you're regressing."

"I'm not regressing," I said in a choked voice, my lungs constricting, working hard to gather some much needed oxygen but it wasn't working. I couldn't breathe, couldn't think, could barely even see as the world around my mother faded and all I could make out were her disapproving eyes glaring up at me. "I'm fine," I wheezed.

"You'd better be, Nell. If I see anything like that again, don't even think for one second that I'll hesitate in sending you back to the institution."

"No," I whispered, desperation making my knees quake. I was ready to beg, to cry until she took it back. "Please," I croaked, reaching my hand out to grip her forearm but she pulled back as soon as I made contact.

"You've been warned, Nell. This is the last time we have this conversation," she said, turning on her heel and disappearing into the dining room.

I slumped against the railing, my breath moving in and out of my lungs in short pants, the air in the house seeming thick, clogged with disapproval and hatred.

Tears collected at the corners of my eyes as I lurched my way up the stairs, my legs shaking so hard that I nearly fell several times.

I can't go back there. I won't.

Finally, I made it to my room and collapsed onto my bed, desperately trying to take deeper breaths, to fill my lungs but it wasn't working.

My mind kept running over all the things she'd said to me and my panic was climbing until my heart felt like it was seizing in my chest.

I moaned and slid to the floor, tears streaming down my face as every muscle in my body cramped up and my body forgot how to breathe, to function.

C'mon Nell, it's not real. You're fine. Breathe. Just breathe.

My vision was going black and my panic wasn't receding. I couldn't get the sight of my mother's enraged face out of my head. My mind swam with it, her words mixing into the anxiety inducing cocktail and for the first time in a long time, I wished for the pills I'd been prescribed, wished I'd taken them so I wouldn't have to feel this pain.

Think, Nell. Use your head, calm down.

Some fragment of sanity managed to penetrate the fog and I began to list the constellations in my head, taking my mind off of the panic as I occupied it with the familiar names.

"Big dipper, little dipper, Cassiopeia, Cepheus, Draco, Orion, Capella, Castor and Pollux, Corona Borealis, Sagittarius, Spica…

I kept going until I managed to suck in a breath between each name and the pain in my chest receded to a dull ache. Angrily, I swiped at the moisture on my cheeks, furious at myself for losing control, for letting it get to that point. It had been so long since I had a panic attack, so long since I fell apart to that extent.

For a moment, I considered staying there, slumped on the floor, my back bowed, my mind and body defeated, my resolution to stop caring a distant memory, stolen away in the span of a few minutes.

Instead, I straightened my spine, tilting my head back as I slowly pieced myself back together, the attack leaving a dull ache in my chest, like a bruise.

I stood up and headed towards my door, intent on getting to the bathroom so I could wash my face but I froze.

Paige stood there, her eyes locked on mine and for a second, I thought I saw pain in their depths and compassion.

Then it was gone and her lips curled into a sneer before she turned her back and walked away from me.

I let out a slow, shaky breath, gritting my teeth against the pain and betrayal adding to the mix of emotions making a home in the pit of my stomach, jumbling my brain.

I walked into the bathroom and turned on the cold water, waiting until it was freezing before I splashed my face with it again and again, hoping it could wake me up.

After a few minutes, I straightened and dried my face, my eyes locked on my reflection, seeing the weariness on my own features, the strain in my own eyes.

It doesn't have to be like this.

My eyes stung at the thought, knowing that it was true but the very thought made me sick to my stomach.

My hand shook as I reached towards the mirror, opening the door to the medicine cabinet and staring hard at the bottles of pills lined up there.

It would be so easy to just take them, to line them up each morning and take each dose like a good little girl, to numb out and forget what it was like to feel things, to want things, to like and dislike things.

I could walk around like the ghost I'd been at the institution. I could watch everything through a veil, never really able to touch anything, to hear anything, to smell anything.

But…

I didn't want that. I hated feeling like that, like I was a zombie walking around in someone else's daydream.

My mind wandered back to earlier, to the feeling that had come over me when Grayson's motorcycle came to life under my hands, when he'd let go of the handlebars and it had been under my control. That was why I didn't take the pills. I wanted to experience everything, even if some of it sucked. I just…needed to get out of my own head sometimes. I needed an escape so the stress of trying to be exactly what my parents wanted me to be didn't weigh on me quite as heavily. I needed Paige to not hate me anymore because she was my rock. She was the only thing that ever made sense.

But I'd lost her, too.

I sucked in a long, deep breath and closed the cabinet, staring at myself in the mirror. "Don't be crazy. Don't screw up," I whispered, knowing that one misstep would open that cabinet wide and my little game would be over.

I couldn't let that happen.

With shaking hands, I pulled the elastic out of my hopelessly tangled and sloppy hair, running my fingers through the strands slowly before tying it back into a low bun, tucking any stray strands into place resolutely.

I'd just avoid him.

My eyes darted nervously around the hallway, my hands clenching my binder until my knuckles were white. My father had given me a ride to school on his way to work and I'd spent the last hour hiding in the library.

Now that homeroom was about to begin, and the halls were milling with students, I had no choice but to brave the real world.

A world with Grayson West in it.

What if he tried to talk to me? What if he thought we were friends now?

I flinched at the thought, fear making my heart beat hard in my chest.

But there was something else there, too. Maybe a hint of…regret?

There were a few moments the day before that had made me think that maybe things between the two of us didn't have to be so hostile, that if we managed to stay civil for a few minutes, we might even get along.

Doesn't matter now.

My hands tightened around my binder again as I thought of my mother's threat and how easy it would be for her to follow through on it. She'd send me away again in a heartbeat. She just needed the perfect excuse and yesterday, I'd pretty much handed it to her on a platter.

Maybe he was skipping today. Maybe I was freaking out for no re——

He was here.

I spotted him down the hallway, his height making him easily visible above the crowd and before I even had a chance to think, our eyes locked and his lips tilted into a crooked grin.

Panic ripped through me the closer he came and I did the only thing I could think of.

I ran.

I literally ran away from him.

Pathetic. I was so damn pathetic.

I only stopped running when I rounded a corner and spotted my class ahead of me. Breathing a sigh of relief, I stepped over the threshold and inside, claiming my seat and placing my supplies neatly across the surface, the familiar act somehow making it easier to breathe.

I didn't see him for the rest of the day and I was just starting to relax when I walked into my sixth period class.

Chemistry. We were in the same chemistry class.

I froze just inside the door, my eyes scanning the nearly empty classroom. I was early, as usual, and briefly, the thought that I could just slip away, skip this class and avoid Grayson, crossed my mind. Of course, I couldn't do that. Skipping wasn't in my DNA.

So, cringing inwardly, I walked towards my desk and, with shaking hands, got my notebook out, lining my pens and pencils up just how I liked them.

"Hey," Craig said, taking the seat beside me.

"Hi," I said in a slightly unsteady voice, sending him a smile that barely touched my lips before it was gone.

"What's wrong?" he asked, his brows lowering slightly as his warm brown eyes narrowing in question.

I shrugged. "Nothing, really. I just…have a lot on my mind."

"Is it your sister?" he asked, leaning a little closer to me.

I shook my head, grabbing a pen so I could neatly write the date at the top of my page. "Nope, this time it's a mess of my own making."

"Hey," he said softly, his voice making my gaze connect firmly with his, seeing the compassion and sincerity in his familiar eyes. "You can talk to me, you know that, right Nell? I know we don't have the most conventional relationship but I consider us friends. I hope you do too."

Something in my chest loosened slightly at the open expression on his face and his sweet words. My throat felt a little tight at the moment so I settled on nodding, keeping my mouth shut because as nice as his words were, I had no intention of unloading on him. He had enough problems without adding mine to the list.

"So, I have an idea," he said after a moment.

"An idea about what?" I asked, raising a brow in his direction.

"I'm thinking that you and I, we need to forget about Brian and Paige for a night."

"I'm not sure that's possible," I said, a wry smile settling across my lips.

"Why don't we give it a shot? I'm having a party on Friday and Brian and Paige are both going to be there. I figure, they're going to drink anyway, right? Might as well be at a party on this side of town where they're less likely to snort anything or take any pills." I winced at the mention of pills, remembering the Klonopin my sister had stolen this past weekend. "I want you to come, Nell. You can relax, let loose a little, while at the same time, keeping half an eye on your sister. What do you say?"

I tried to keep my expression polite but inside, I was already saying no. "It's not exactly my scene, Craig."

"What are you talking about? It's my house and I'm inviting you. Of course it's your scene."

I shrugged. "I don't party."

"I'm not saying you have to get smashed. Just come over, shoot some pool and have some fun. You know you're going to end up there anyway to pick her up. Just come a little earlier this time."

I gave a light chuckle at his accurate assumption. "I'll think about it," I said, glancing at the clock to see that the bell was about to ring and the class was nearly full.

Grayson West hadn't arrived yet.

A faint feeling of hope made the nerves in the pit of my stomach calm slightly. Maybe he wouldn't show up? Maybe he was skipping?

I looked down at my desk, pushing a highlighter just a bit so that it was in line with the others before glancing up at the clock again just as the bell rang.

I let out a sigh of relief, my spine losing some of its stiffness as my lips lifted slightly in the corners, happy that at least for now, I didn't have to face Grayson West.

It was just as that thought crossed my mind that he walked in, his stride unhurried, his expression unapologetic as he looked straight at Mr. Wright before heading towards his desk.

I kept my head down, my hand clenched hard around one of my pens as he walked closer towards me. Of course his desk had to be at the back and of course he had to walk right next to me to get to it.

I wasn't breathing and every step he took seemed to echo in my head. God, was he walking in slow motion? What was taking so long?

Oh wait, he wasn't walking at all.

My gaze shifted slightly to the side to see a pair of shoes at a standstill right next to my desk.

Go away, go away, go away…

He didn't go away.

Instead, he leaned closer to me, planting his hands on the edges of my desk until our faces were barely a hairsbreadth away from each other.

"Take a seat, Mr. West," Mr. Wright said.

"Is that it, Cupcake?" Grayson said, his voice so low and quiet that I was the only one who could hear him.

My eyes were on his chin and the nerves in my stomach had multiplied exponentially. "Sit down," I hissed through clenched teeth.

He didn't. Instead, he reached out, and with two fingers, he lifted my chin until I was forced to meet his gaze.

Everything inside of me froze as our eyes connected and locked. He looked furious. Like if I said one wrong word, he'd snap and god only knew what would happen next.

"Is that it, Nell?"

"Mr. West, either take a seat or get out of my class, now!" Mr. Wright shouted.

I barely heard him, the only thing penetrating the fog in my brain at the moment was the sound of Grayson asking me that question.

"Is that it?" he repeated, something barely restrained in his tone, on the verge of dangerous.

I felt frozen in place, our gazes locked on each other, his fingers still on my chin. Finally, with what I hoped was a blank expression and a steady voice, I whispered, "Yes."

Then it was gone. His touch, the weight of his stare, the questions in his eyes. It was all just...gone leaving nothing but a blank look of indifference.

His eyes shifted to the pens lined up on my desk, and slowly, he reached out and shifted the one on the very end until it was just slightly out of order before moving on towards the back of the classroom.

"What the hell was that?" Craig whispered close to my ear as Mr. Wright began the lecture.

I just shook my head, my eyes locked on that one pen that was different than the rest, the one that didn't quite line up.

The longer I stared at it, the tighter the coil in my chest got until my palms started to sweat and my heart pounded in my ears.

Feeling like I'd lost something, like I'd been playing a game without knowing the rules, I reached out and straightened the pen, lining it up perfectly once more.

The rest of the week went by quickly and even though I half expected another run in with Grayson, none came.

I saw him occasionally, and each time, my heart rate would increase and nerves would seep into my skin, making my breath hitch a bit but then his eyes would just drift over me, like he didn't even notice I was there.

Good. This is perfect.

I was back to being invisible to him, back to being the Nell that nobody bothered to pay attention to, the Nell that didn't ride on motorcycles and definitely didn't get lessons on how to drive them from Grayson West.

It was better this way. I never lost my temper, never said anything I didn't mean or didn't think about first. Now that Grayson West was out of my life for good, I had my control back.

This is how it's supposed to be.

So what if it didn't feel quite as comfortable as it had before, like slipping back into my old routine didn't exactly...fit right anymore.

The feeling was just temporary. I just needed to focus on school, on finding a new job, on staying under everyone's radar.

"Don't tell me you're worried about your hair," Paige said, leaning her shoulder against my doorframe, giving me a once over before twisting her lips into a cruel grin that looked ugly on her pretty face. "No one's going to be looking at you anyway, Nellie. Craig only invited you out of pity."

I frowned, running my fingers through my loose waves, half shocked at how long it was. I so rarely kept it down that I was surprised to see how much it had grown and even though it looked kind of…nice down, I didn't think I could handle it like that for the whole night. Already, when I moved too much, or breathed a certain way, the shifting of my hair threw me off, distracted me and made me want to tie it up in its familiar low bun.

"Hurry up, will you? Brian wants to get going." She turned her back on me but stopped only a step away from my bedroom door. "Just tie it back, Nell. You know you're going to anyway," she said, casting a patronizing look over her shoulder before moving down the hallway and out of my sight.

Anger churned in my gut and even though my fingers itched to smooth the strands back into a bun, I refused the impulse and left my hair loose, dangling around my shoulders and down my back.

It was just hair, right?

Tearing my eyes away from the mirror, I grabbed my purse and walked out of my room, ignoring the way my hair was falling into my face, tickling my skin uncomfortably.

"Oh god," Paige groaned when she caught sight of me, rolling her eyes before she pushed open the front door. "Ready?" she asked, reaching back to link her hand with Brian's whose eyes were locked on me.

"Well, well, someone put in an effort," Brian said, grinning at me, his eyes already a bit watery and bloodshot. "Who's it for, Nellie? Who are you trying to impress?"

"No one," I said softly, gritting my teeth at how weak I sounded, how scared. God, did I have no backbone? Why couldn't I just tell him to fuck off, to shut up or find a different way to the party?

"I don't believe that for a second," Brian said as we all left the house and I turned around to lock the door behind us. My parents were out of town for the weekend so the place would be empty for the next few hours.

"Believe it," I muttered, turning the key in the lock.

"Is it Craig?" Brian said, suddenly much closer to me, his hand on my hip, his mouth brushing my ear as he spoke.

I stiffened, my spine going ramrod straight as my heart pounded uncomfortably in my chest. "N-no," I stuttered, trying to pull away but his hand tightened on my waist, keeping me in place.

"No?" he whispered, bringing his chest flush against my back. "Then is it…me?"

I wanted to throw up, to punch him, to scream, anything but stand there in shocked silence, my brain shifting into overdrive as he seemed to press ever closer to me.

"Stop messing with her, Bri," Paige said, her tone filled with boredom and a hint of irritation. "If she has a panic attack, she can't give us a ride."

Brian tilted his head back and laughed, pulling his hands away from me before wrapping his arm around my sister's shoulders and dragging her towards my car. "But it's so much fun, babe!"

I gritted my teeth as rage temporarily swamped me. Fun? It was fun to fuck with me? Fun to push my buttons, to drive me crazy, to make me feel like a complete idiot?

"Why don't you go play in traffic?" I said under my breath, my voice barely audible but Brian stopped in his tracks anyway.

"What was that, Nell?" he asked as I turned to face them, my eyes meeting his steadily for once, my spine straight.

"Let's just go to this stupid party," I mumbled, brushing past them and wrenching the driver's side door open, settling in and starting the engine which turned over immediately for once.

Torture. This was going to be pure torture, I could tell.

Why the hell had I let Craig talk me into this? I could've just shown up at the end of the night like I usually did and dragged Paige home like any other day.

Or better yet, I could've just left her there. She could've crashed at Craig's for the night so I could have the night off.

Instead, I found myself parking my car on Craig's street, wincing at all the cars lined up nearby.

Too many people.

Trepidation eased its way under my skin, settling there like an entire-body sliver.

"Wait in the car until we get in, okay? I don't want to be seen going to a party with my freak of a sister," Paige said, giggling obnoxiously.

"You know what?" I snapped, undoing my seatbelt and climbing out of the car before leaning my head back in to glare at the ungrateful little twit. Who was this girl? "Why don't you guys wait? I'm going inside."

With that, I slammed the car door, not even caring that the whole vehicle shuddered and creaked from the impact.

I was too busy fuming to realize how close to the house I'd gotten and before I focused, I was already turning the doorknob and stepping inside.

My heart stalled and my throat closed as a few people standing nearby looking my way, one girl rolling her eyes and sending me a sneer before she turned on her heel and marched deeper into the house.

This was a mistake.

My lungs were burning before I remembered to take a breath and even then, it was short and choppy, providing little to no relief for the panic that was climbing up my throat and choking me.

I was about to turn around and leave when Craig was suddenly there, his hands on my shoulders, his eyes locked on mine. "Hey," he said, giving me a soft smile, filled with understanding. "Let's go downstairs."

I blinked a few times when he reached down and took my hand in his, leading me through the hallways, occasionally pausing to say hi to a friend but never stopping for longer than a few seconds. I kept my head down, feeling people's eyes on me, wondering what the hell I was doing there and why in the world was golden boy Craig holding my hand?

"You good?" he asked once we'd made it to the basement which was the man cave of the house. The dart board, pool table, big screen TV, and intense sound system had attracted quite a few other people but at least it wasn't as crowded down there as it had been upstairs.

"Yeah," I said, trying to keep my voice firm.

His brow rose and his chocolate eyes warmed. "Really?"

I sighed and ran a hand through my loose hair, wincing at the feel of the strands running through my fingers. "No. I shouldn't have come here. This isn't me, Craig. I don't——"

"Hey," he said, cutting me off and planting his hands on my shoulders, forcing me to meet his gaze squarely. "I want you here. It's your turn to have a little fun for once, okay? Can you just let go for a minute? Just one little minute?"

No.

I shrugged and planted a shaky smile on my lips. "I can try."

His mouth spread into a wide grin and he gripped my hand again, pulling me towards the pool table. "C'mon, let's play a game."

I gave a short laugh. "I don't play pool, Craig."

"I'll teach you," he said, setting up the balls at one end of the table, lining them up before pulling the plastic triangle thing away from them. "Do you want to break?"

"You're kidding, right?" I grumbled, taking the cue he was holding out to me.

He chuckled and proceeded to show me the basics of holding the cue and lining up your shot. I paid attention but I knew this wasn't going to be pretty.

"Okay, your turn," he said, once he'd broken, sending the balls flying in all directions. He'd taken a couple more shots after that, telling me that he was solids so I had to aim for stripes.

Right. Aim.

I picked a likely ball and leaned over the table, eying the cue ball with trepidation. I'd count it as a good shot if I even managed to hit the thing.

I did, but the ball went in entirely the wrong direction, sending a different stripe into a corner pocket.

He was silent for a second. "That was awesome, Nell."

"It was just luck," I mumbled, moving away from the table.

"It's still your shot."

With a sigh, I lined up the next shot, wincing when the cue hit the white ball a little crookedly, sending it on a weird angle that made it hit the bank before it connected with another ball, sending it into a side pocket.

"I thought you said you've never played!" Craig said, narrowing his eyes at me from across the table.

"I haven't!" I said, frowning down at my next shot.

This time, the white ball flew off the table, landing on the ground and rolling until it hit the wall.

"See," I said, smothering a chuckle as Craig tilted his back and laughed openly.

"Okay, I believe you." He reached for the ball and placed it on the table, sending a smirk my way. "Just try not to hit any windows, okay?"

I rolled my eyes, leaning against the wall as he took another shot. "I'll try my hardest."

It took him about five minutes to thoroughly beat me at pool.

"You weren't that bad," Craig said as I placed my cue on the rack.

"Yeah, right," I muttered, my lips stretching into a small smile. I'd sucked but it hadn't been that bad. It was almost…fun.

"C'mon," Craig said, placing his hand over mine, halting my movements. "Let's play aga——"

"I'm playing the winner!" one of Craig's friends interrupted, bumping his shoulder into me, knocking me back a couple of steps.

I took a couple more steps back in order to avoid the big guy and his sloppy movements. He seemed pretty drunk and his girlfriend was sidling over towards me with a malicious look in her eyes.

I gritted my teeth and hastily glanced around the room, looking for a conveniently located exit.

"I'm just going to——"

"Find someone else to play with," Craig said to his friend, gripping my wrist lightly before pulling me towards the stairs. "C'mon, Nell, I'm giving you the grand tour."

I blinked down at his hand holding me gently, confused. "What are you doing, Craig," I asked quietly, my voice barely a squeak, yet despite the volume in the house, he somehow managed to hear me.

We were in the kitchen and there were quite a few people in there, mixing drinks and pouring beer. "I'm just showing you around, Nell."

I shook my head lightly, trying to make my shoulders smaller as people brushed against me, making my skin prickle at the proximity of all the bodies pressing against me. "That's not what I meant," I whispered, my breath hitching as a girl purposefully bumped into me, making me stumble slightly.

"Watch it!" Craig shouted at the girl who barely even paused at the sound of his voice. "Come on. I'll show you the upstairs."

I shook my head but followed him anyway because the lower level was too packed. All the oxygen was being used by people who hated me.

When we reached the top of the stairs, I shook my head lightly, trying to clear the static scratching through my brain. "Craig, I don't think this was a good——"

"You're my friend, Nell," Craig said, coming to a sudden stop, turning towards me with a serious expression on his face. His usually warm, chocolate brown eyes were sharper, a little bit darker and his expression was hard. "I'm sick of the way people treat you. If I want to invite you to a party, I will. It's none of their damn business."

My lips parted but I didn't know what to say to that, so I remained silent as he led me towards a bedroom. "This is my room," he said, walking inside, leaving the door open behind us.

It was huge and a little bit messy but it reminded me of him. There were pictures and books and CDs all over the place not to mention about a million trophies from all his various accomplishments. I ran my fingers over one trophy of a baseball player with the letter MVP on the bottom. "I don't want them to judge you for spending time with me, Craig." My eyes went unfocused as my fingers continued to trace those three letters on the little gold plaque. "I'm used to the way they look at me but you..." I shook my head slightly, turning towards him, trying to explain. "I don't want them to look at you like that. You've spent so much energy trying to help Brian, the last thing you need is to add me to the list."

"I don't care what they think about me, Nell," he said, taking a couple steps closer to me. "Wait," he said, reaching out to grip my wrist. "I like it down."

I frowned, realizing I'd been in the process of smoothing my hair back into its usual low bun. A sick feeling swirled in my stomach, hating how hard it was for me to be normal, even just for a few minutes.

"Nell?" I blinked up at Craig, letting my hair fall from my fingers. His hand was still on my wrist, cradling my skin lightly as my hand lowered.

"Yeah?" I said, confused at the expression on his face. I'd never seen him look at me like that before.

He opened his mouth to reply but before he got the chance, the sound of footsteps stopping at the door to his bedroom halted his words.

"Well, this is cozy."

I felt the colour drain from my face at the sound of his voice, my head automatically swinging towards him as my stomach dropped.

What was he doing here?

"What the hell are you doing here, West?" Craig said, his voice low and filled with barely restrained anger. My gaze was drawn back to him in surprise. I'd never heard him sound like that before.

"You act like you don't want me here," Grayson said, his tone easy but as soon as he took a step into the room, the tension in the atmosphere ratcheted up several notches. "I'm hurt."

"Get out of my house," Craig said, turning towards Grayson, not letting go of my wrist.

"Now, now, whatever happened to hospitality?" Grayson said, his tone still calm but his dark eyes were a swirling mass of anger as they shifted to me. His expression was smooth, totally blank but there was something in the way he held his chin, in the way that muscle in his jaw jumped every once in a while that told me he wasn't exactly feeling serene. "You're still here, Cupcake? I would've thought you'd be running away by now."

I gritted my teeth, a part of me wishing I could give him some sort of explanation, but what was I supposed to say? I was afraid that my parents would send me to an institution if I was civil to him?

Yeah, way to sound normal, Nell.

"Just drop it, Grayson," I settled on, my eyes darting to the floor, unable to meet his dark gaze as he continued to stare at me.

"Come on, Cupcake. I thought we were becoming friends," he spat, his tone loaded with sarcasm. "Maybe I don't want to drop it."

"Nell would never be friends with someone like you, West," Craig snapped, taking a step closer to Grayson.

"Of course not," Grayson snapped back, his eyes narrowing on Craig. "She's too fucking perfect to associate with someone like me, right? My filth might rub off on her if she stands too close."

"Stop it!" I half shouted, ripping my wrist out of Craig's hold and closing the distance between me and Grayson, plating my hands on his chest and giving an ineffectual shove. "How many times do I have to tell you I'm not perfect? Not even fucking close, Grayson."

"Obviously not," he snarled, bringing his face closer to mine. "Do me a favour, Cupcake. Next time you want to go slumming, don't look at me, okay?"

I ground my teeth together, too angry to form words. My hands were clenched so hard at my sides that my fingernails were digging into my skin.

"And you," I blinked, hearing a darker tone in his voice as he addressed Craig and in two quick steps, he was in front of him, Grayson's arm across Craig's throat as he slammed him against a bookshelf, knocking a few trophies to the floor. I watched as Grayson leaned in closer and said something in Craig's ear that was too low for me to hear but it made Craig's face drain of colour before Grayson let him go abruptly.

Then, without a backward glance, Grayson left the room and pounded his way down the stairs.

What the...?

"Are you okay?" I asked Craig, finding it hard to focus past the fury raging in my veins. What was his problem? Slumming? He thought I was just some bitch who was looking for a ride on the back of his motorcycle? He had no fucking clue who I was. He had no idea what kind of person I was. How dare he accuse me of something like that?

Craig nodded, straightening his spine and taking a step towards me. "You need to stay away from that guy, Nell."

I nodded distractedly, my eyes on the door to his bedroom. "Yeah. Listen, I'm going to leave. Make sure Paige stays here tonight, okay?"

"What? You just got here!"

"Yeah. I need to leave. Thanks for inviting me, Craig," I said as I walked out of his room and headed down the stairs, not even noticing the evil glares I was getting from the other partygoers as I bee-lined it towards the front door.

When I was on the lawn, I spotted Grayson with his friend, Dan looking into the open hood of a car.

My eyes trailed over to where my beat up old car sat and back towards them as I told myself to just drop it, to move on but I found my feet taking me towards them, my rage propelling me and building steam with every step.

"Hey!" I shouted when I got closer, making both their gazes swing towards me. I didn't stop walking until I was chest to chest with Grayson, adrenaline flowing in my veins. "Screw you, Grayson West. You know what? You can act like you know everything all you want but you are never going to know me, so don't pretend like you do."

"I'm just looking at the facts, Cupcake," he snarled, not backing up an inch. "You're the one who literally ran away from me at school. What am I supposed to think? You didn't sprint in the other direction because I had spinach in my teeth."

"It had nothing to do with you," I snapped, glaring up at him.

He snorted and rolled his eyes. "You can't be serious. How much of an idiot do you think I am?"

I shook my head, trying to clear it but it only seemed to get more muddled.

"Don't even try to tell me it had nothing to do with me, Cupcake. It's written all over your face. Your mom said something to you. Did she ground you for being with me? Was she disappointed in her daughter because she spent time with a guy like me?" his voice was low and even as he took a step towards me, forcing me back a step. "Maybe she took away your cell phone or threatened to cut off your allowance? It's okay, Nell. I get it. You don't want to disappoint your parents, right? It must be a lot to live up to, having parents who could afford a mansion like theirs, who have everything. Do they know how much of a screw up Paige is? Is that why you need to act like a little robot all the time?"

"She's not a screw up," I snapped.

He scoffed. "You're in denial, Cupcake. But, you're right, it's none of my business. You do whatever you want with your life and I'll do whatever I want with mine. I wouldn't want to stress you out or anything so I won't be talking to you again."

"Perfect," I hissed through gritted teeth, turning my back on him and heading towards my car. I could feel his eyes on me the whole time, and when I looked back, he was still looking at me with an odd expression on his face before it went blank and he raised a brow as if asking why I was still there.

Emotions were swirling in my gut in an odd mixture of panic, anger, and...hurt that didn't sit well.

I turned back towards my car and reached for the door handle, my hand closing around it and tugging, the door screeching open painfully.

Before I stepped in, I looked over my shoulder to see Dan and Grayson hunched over the car, trying to solve the puzzle of why the thing wouldn't start and before I realized what I was doing, my mouth was open and I was asking, "Do you guys need a ride?"

Grayson just looked at me like I was crazy but Dan grinned and said, "That would be awesome, Nell!" before slamming the hood of his car closed and jogging towards me. "You're a lifesaver," he said, still grinning as he chucked me under the chin then climbed into the back seat of my car. "You coming, West?" he shouted out of the back window, apparently oblivious to the tension between his friend and me.

Slowly, Grayson began to walk towards me, his eyes never once leaving mine as he closed the distance between us, stopping barely a foot in front of me. The muscle in his jaw twitched as he stared down at me, anger swirling in his dark eyes. "What game are you playing, Nell?" he growled.

I shook my head but before I got the chance to say anything, Dan half-shouted. "What the hell are you talking about? Just get in the damn car so we can go home." Then, in a much quieter voice, he mumbled, "I never wanted to come to this damn party in the first place," before rolling up the window.

My brows lowered in question as I focused on Grayson once more but he was already turning away from me and rounding the front of my car, heading towards the passenger side.

I frowned as I got behind the wheel and closed the door before starting the car. What did Dan mean he hadn't wanted to come to the party? Did he mean Grayson wanted to? And why in the world would Grayson West want to go to Craig's party?

I frowned as I moved forward, barely even registering that my car had started on the first try which was usually cause for celebration.

I followed Dan's directions without thought, going through the motions of driving without really paying attention. I was lucky that it was late and there were hardly any cars on the street because with all the tension in the air between me and Grayson, concentration was not something I could pull off at the moment.

"This is me!" Dan said when I'd pulled up to a small house on a street I didn't recognize. "Thanks, Nell. You're a gem!" he said before climbing out of the car and slamming the door, making the whole frame groan. Jeez, was he entirely made up of muscle?

We sat there in silence for a long moment after Dan had disappeared inside of his house.

"Where do I go?" I asked, my voice embarrassingly weak.

"What, you don't remember how to get to my neighbourhood, Cupcake?"

I gritted my teeth and shook my head.

He sent me a flat look before pointing in the right direction. "That way."

I nodded and put the car into reverse, pulling out into the street, my hands gripping the steering wheel so tightly that my knuckles were white.

He didn't say anything unless he was giving me directions and the tension in the vehicle only increased until we finally came to a stop in front of his house.

"Thanks for the ride," he said without looking at me, his voice laced with disdain and sarcasm as he opened the door.

Good. That was perfect. Once he was out of my car, I could go back to figuring out my own shit and not have to worry about what Grayson West thought of me or why Grayson West would to go to a party that none of his friends would be at.

This was great.

"Wait."

I blinked, hearing the word that had slipped out of my mouth, feeling his wrist as I gripped it in the hand I'd unintentionally reached out to him to get him to stop.

He turned towards me with an eyebrow quirked and a bored expression on his face. "What is it now, Cupcake?"

"I..." I trailed off, knowing what I wanted to say even if I didn't really want to say it, one side of me warring with the other. In my head, I could hear my mother's voice, telling me to stay away from Grayson but it was faint, drowned out almost completely by the hard beating of my heart and the racing of the blood in my veins.

"Listen, Cupcake, it's getting late so if you don't have anything to say..."

"God, you really don't make this easy, do you?" I said through gritted teeth.

His eyebrow rose further. "Why the hell would I make anything easy for a girl that can't stand to be civil to me? You'll have to excuse me, Cupcake but I'm not one of those guys from the wrong side of town who wags his tail for any rich bitch who might show him the time of day. I was nice to you and you threw it in my face so thanks for the ride but——"

"I'm sorry, okay?" I half shouted, the words so laced with anger that any sincerity I may have felt was gone. "That's what I wanted to say, that's why I stopped you from leaving the car and that's why I followed you out of Craig's house." I shook my head, running a hand through my hair as I gave a short laugh. "Only now, I'm wondering why I even bothered."

He snorted. "Was that supposed to be an apo——"

"Just shut up for a second, okay?" I snapped, a part of me surprised at the way I was talking to him but another part of me was starting to get used to it, to like the way words rolled off my tongue when Grayson was around. I took a deep breath and met his gaze squarely this time when I said, "I'm sorry," in a low, clear voice, devoid of anger. "I shouldn't have run from you at school the way I did. You're right. You were nice to me and I...was a bitch," I said, cringing at the memory of the way I'd panicked when I saw him. "You were right about my mom, too. She did say something when I got home that day but it's not my allowance on the line," I said, my voice getting smaller as I thought about the institute and what it would mean for me to go back there. "It's more," I said softly, my gaze locked on his. "It's a lot more than that."

For a long, drawn out moment, we just sat there, staring at each other, the cool wind from his open door making goosebumps rise on my arms but I didn't move.

I watched as something began to swirl in his eyes, an emotion that, at first, was indistinguishable but the more I looked at him, the clearer it became. He was angry.

"So, what you're saying," he began, his voice low and controlled but I sensed an edge of that anger buried beneath his cool tone, "is you're sorry, but you can't be seen with me in public. Am I right?"

I winced, wishing I could argue with him on this one but he wasn't wrong.

He gave a short, humourless laugh. "What happened to the Nell I saw the other day? The one that didn't give a shit what her parents thought? The one that wanted to be seen with me in front of her mom?"

I shook my head, feeling my throat close a little at the thought of the threat that loomed over my head now. "You don't understand," I croaked.

"Then explain it to me, Cupcake."

I blinked, my mind rebelling at the suggestion. Explain it to him? Tell him that I was afraid that if my mother ever saw me on the back of his motorcycle or anywhere near him again, I'd be back in the one place that I never wanted to go again. Ever.

Yeah, I wasn't telling him that.

"I-I..." I trailed off, whatever words I may have spoken dead before they even reached my lips. What was I supposed to tell him? That I was a coward? That even though I hated it, I couldn't help but feel panicked at the thought of disappointing my parents?

It didn't matter anyway. Grayson's gaze cleared and his face relaxed until he looked totally carefree and completely in control. His eyes focused on me and there was no anger in their depths as he gave me a cool stare. "You know what? Forget it. None of this matters anyway, does it Nell? It's obvious to anyone looking. You and I," he gestured between the two of us with a careless wave of his hand, "aren't meant to be friends." He shrugged and his gaze hardened as he leaned a little closer to me, his mask of indifference making something in my stomach churn painfully. "Thinking back, I get the feeling I'd be far better off without your friendship, anyway. Don't you agree?" he asked, giving a sardonic twist of his lips before stepping out of my car and slamming the door shut without another word.

I sat there for a while, staring at the last spot I'd seen him, walking calmly away from me, disappearing into his house, going back to his own world. A world I had no place in.

And no matter how many times I told myself that this was a good thing, that I didn't need Grayson in my life, I couldn't help but think that no matter how much we fought and how many times I lost control around him, there was a part of me that felt…at ease when he was around. Like I could just be Nell.

I shook my head, putting my car into reverse and leaving Grayson's house behind. What was I thinking? It didn't matter who was looking at me, or talking to me, or aggravating me, I could never just be Nell.

I'd tried that before and all I'd managed to do was completely alienate my family.

From now on, I'd forget about the Nell who argued with dangerous guys, who offered said guys a ride home and who laughed at the exhilaration of learning to drive a motorcycle.

I'd forget about her because that Nell…

She just wasn't good enough.

Chapter 6

Chapter 6

I squinted down at the paper in front of me, biting my lip as I reconsidered my wording in the conclusion. It seemed smooth and it flowed nicely. I'd spent an entire week editing the damn thing, painstakingly going over each and every detail until it was as polished as it was going to get.

Still...

Was it enough?

The last time I'd given Mr. Ford a paper, he'd given me an A minus. He'd told me to work harder.

Hah.

Well, this paper was pretty damn near perfect. I'd done extra reading, scouring the library until I'd found every single book on the subject, forgoing sleep so I didn't miss anything.

So I never had to see another minus again.

If he had a problem with my paper this time, maybe it wasn't my writing that bothered him.

Maybe it was just me.

Wouldn't be the first time, I thought as my father walked into the kitchen and opened the fridge, not even once glancing in my direction. I sat on a stool at the island in the centre of the open concept kitchen. I was pretty hard to miss.

"Good morning," I said, my voice soft, as if I was afraid any loud noise might startle him, might make him realize the resident pariah was in the same room as him.

He just grunted, pouring himself a cup of coffee and grabbing a muffin before taking a seat across from me.

Well, he sat sort of diagonally from me.

As in, the furthest seat he could be from me.

My chest tightened slightly and I felt my heart stutter a bit before resuming at a faster pace, making my breathing pick up.

I bit my lip as I discretely studied my father while he read the paper, wondering what it was that made this so hard for us. Why was it that other families existed together with such ease? They laughed and watched cartoons and had actual conversations. What was it about me that made it so difficult?

You're crazy.

My eyes came to rest on my paper again and I winced inwardly, seeing the way the bottom of the pages lined up perfectly with the edge of the counter and the way my muffin was cut into four equal parts so precise that they looked almost measured.

I cleared my throat trying to ignore the way my heart was racing as I stood to get a glass of water. "Dad, would you like a———"

"Morning, Daddy," Paige said, waltzing into the kitchen and planting a kiss on my father's cheek. I watched, frozen, as his eyes lit up and the wrinkles that had been bunching his forehead smoothed out.

"Morning, Paige," he said warmly. "Tell me," he continued, turning his attention back to the newspaper as Paige made a bowl of cereal, ignoring me, "are you planning on actually attending school today?"

Paige shrugged, sending a grin over her shoulder towards my dad. "I hadn't decided yet."

He chuckled lightly, shaking his head before turning the page.

"What the hell are you doing, freak?"

I blinked at Paige, realizing that she was staring at me as I held a glass clutched in my fingers, close to my chest, holding it as if it were precious.

It was precious. At that moment, that glass in my hands, felt like the only thing keeping me sane, the only thing that kept me from screaming at my father, begging him to explain to me why, why he couldn't look at me like that? Why was it so hard for him to see past the girl who'd spent a summer in a fucking asylum? Why was it so hard for him to even look at me at all?

"Get out of my way, loser," Paige grumbled, pushing her way past me to grab the milk from the fridge.

I felt the brush of her shoulder as if it was a match and I was made of pure gasoline. I jerked away from her, feeling her disdainful glare as I rushed around the island, reaching a hand out to collect my paper before booking it out of that damn kitchen.

For an open concept, there sure as shit wasn't enough air in the space.

I was moving at a good clip, sucking in deep breaths of air when I took a corner too tightly and tripped over a table leg, losing my balance and slamming into the hardwood floor. The glass I'd still been holding shattered around me and I winced as I felt a shard slice the palm of my left hand.

My breath came in short wheezy pants as I knelt there, frozen, staring at the shards of glass scattered across the floor.

"Oh no," I moaned, my panic skyrocketing as I reached out and began to sweep the glass towards me, trying to make a smaller pile and cutting myself more in the process.

"What the hell are you doing?" I heard my mother shriek from behind me.

"I'm sorry," I whispered, my lack of air keeping me from speaking at a higher volume.

I blinked when her hand wrapped around my left wrist, making me go completely still. "You're just making it worse, Nell!" she said, her voice laced with fury as she glared at me. "Clean yourself up then take care of this mess. Use your head, for once," she hissed, her hand releasing mine abruptly.

I nodded, swallowing repeatedly, trying to keep the panic at bay even as the edges of my vision began to go dark and my lungs strained for more oxygen. "I-I'm sorry," I croaked as I stood, trying to keep my expression impassive as I faced her. "I'll c-c-clean this up in a m-minute," I said, cringing at the way I stuttered.

Keep it together, Nell. Just keep it together long enough to get out of here.

I straightened my spine, trying to seem normal as I turned away from my mother but her eyes were on me the whole time, burning holes in my skin wherever they rested. I could feel her inspecting me, searching for the flaws, cataloguing each piece of evidence that marked me as unconditionally crazy.

I wanted to laugh at the thought.

Of course she didn't need more proof. Sylvia gave her notes to my parents at the end of every month and judging by the amount of pills she kept giving me, those notes didn't mention anything about how much I was improving.

I hurried into my bathroom and slammed the door behind me, sinking onto the tile floor as soon as the lock clicked.

Breathe, Nell. Please, just breathe.

It wasn't working. It was going to happen again. I could feel it in the way my chest kept tightening, in the way my lungs were burning, in the way my skin felt like it was on fire.

"No," I moaned, clenching my hands into fists at my sides, making the blood pour more quickly from my wounds, spilling onto the floor.

Reaching up, I planted one hand on my chest, right above my heart, willing it to slow. "C'mon," I croaked, slumping sideways until my cheek was resting against the cool floor. I took in a deep breath, closing my eyes so I could picture the constellations clearly. "B-big dipper," I began, waiting until I had enough oxygen to say the next. "Cassiopeia."

I ran through the list twice before I could breathe normally again.

Five minutes later, my hands were covered in bandages and my heart felt a little bruised but at least I could breathe well enough to clean up my mess.

I walked down the stairs and found a broom to sweep up the broken glass, realizing quickly that I was going to have to mop, too. There were smears of blood all over the hardwood, making it look a little like someone got murdered right there.

I looked fleetingly at the paper for Mr. Ford's class, noting the blood covered front page. I'd have to reprint that before I left for school.

My head snapped up at the thought, my eyes latching onto the nearest clock.

I was going to be late.

My breath whooshed out of me at the thought, knowing that Mr. Ford didn't accept late papers. Only a doctor's note would excuse you and even then, you pretty much had to be dying to get an extension.

I didn't think a few scrapes on the palms of my hands would qualify me.

"I have to go," I whispered to the remnants of my mess on the floor, rushing through the rest of the clean-up, all the while begging the clock to stop ticking, feeling my panic begin to rise again. "I'll make it," I whispered, urging myself to move faster as I raced up the stairs and reprinted my paper, tapping my fingers as the pages crawled out of the printer.

Once the paper was securely in my bag, I glanced at my reflection in the mirror and froze. My hair was a mess, the bun tilted to the side and strands of loose hair floating all over my head but what caught my attention most was the bloody handprint right in the middle of my chest.

"Oh my god," I muttered, ripping my shirt off and placing it in the laundry basket, pulling the first shirt I saw hanging in my closet over my head.

I sprinted to my car after that, sending up a silent prayer the whole time that the stupid thing would just start on the first try, that it would just bring me to school without a hitch.

"If you work today," I whispered, approaching the rusted vehicle, "I promise to never bitch about you again. I promise I will use the best oil on your hinges and the finest gasoline that money can buy," I muttered, climbing into the car, wincing at the screech my door let out as I closed it. "Please, please, please…" I begged as I placed the key in the ignition and held my breath.

Miraculously, the engine turned over and I laughed as I pulled out of the driveway. I glanced at the clock on the dash and my grin widened when I realized I would be on time. So the day had gotten off to kind of a rocky start but this paper was perfect and as long as I got it to Mr. Ford at the start of class, he'd have no choice but to give me an A.

I pulled into the school parking lot five minutes before the bell would ring and after smoothing my hair back into its usual low bun, I hurried into the building, arriving at my locker with three minutes to spare.

I just needed to grab my——

Someone bumped into my side, cutting off my thought process and dumping a full cup of coffee onto my chest and the books I was holding in my hands.

"Oh shit, I'm so sorry! I wasn't even loo…king," her voice trailed off as her eyes came to rest on my face. I recognized her. She was friends with Paige. "Oh," she said, a knowing smile lifting the corners of her mouth as any apology that had been in her eyes faded. "You're not going to have a breakdown about this, are you?" she sneered before patting me on the arm and brushing past me. "Better get cleaned up, Nell. The bell's about to ring.

I stood there, stunned, coffee dripping down my clothes and off my books onto the floor. "Oh my god," I muttered when I realized that my paper, my paper that I'd worked so hard on, that I'd already had to reprint once today, was in that pile of books.

"Stay calm," I whispered, kneeling on the ground and spreading out my books with shaking fingers. "It's probably fine."

My hand came to rest on the now unrecognizable cover page, the paper tearing as my fingers brushed over it. "No, no, no, no," I whimpered, my throat closing as my heart began to hammer in my chest.

Oh god, I was screwed. Mr. Ford didn't take late papers.

Mr. Ford didn't take late papers.

I'd fail. Forget the A minus, I'd get a zero on this paper. If I got a zero...

I shook my head, trying not the think about it as I frantically collected my books and began walking towards class, telling myself that it would be fine, that he'd be able to see, clearly, that I had the paper ready but it had been destroyed. I'd just show him its remains and I'd bring him a good copy by the end of the day.

He'd understand.

He had to understand.

The bell rang just as I stepped into the classroom, my shoes squeaking on the tile floor. I could feel the class watching me as I walked towards Mr. Ford's desk, but I didn't pay them any attention. I was focused on him. I just needed to explain so that my heart would stop beating so hard, so that I could take a deep breath and my chest could stop aching.

"M-Mr. Ford," I wheezed, stopping in front of his desk, drawing his gaze from the slip of paper he'd been reading. His eyes widened as they took me in.

"Nell? What happened?"

"S-someone spilled coffee on me. I-I have my p-paper," I muttered, holding out the soggy mess that had once been my perfect essay.

"Nell," Mr. Ford said, eyeing my work with disgust, not even bothering to take it from me. "That's not a paper. It's a napkin."

I shook my head as my ears started to ring, gritting my teeth against a wave of nausea that swept through me. "I had it, though," I croaked. "It's done. I just need to reprint it."

His brow cocked as he looked at me. "You want me to give you extra time, Nell?"

I shook my head, frowning as the ringing in my ears turned to a dull roar. "No. Yes. I just...need to go home and reprint it. I'll have it to you by the end of the day."

"You know my policy on late papers."

My hand holding the paper started to shake. "It's not late. It's right here," I hissed, putting my books down so I could flip the front page of the paper, trying to force him to look at it, to give it a chance.

His eyes narrowed and a hint of irritation entered his gaze. "I can't accept that paper, Nell. If you don't have a different one to give me, then I'm afraid you'll have to take a zero for this one."

My heart stopped and I felt the colour drain from my cheeks. "Zero?" I repeated faintly, vaguely hearing the class laughing at me.

"You know my policy. You should've been more careful."

I blinked. "Careful?" I croaked.

He nodded, gesturing his head towards the desks. "Now take a seat, Miss Watson. Class has begun."

I didn't move. I couldn't. My feet were frozen in place, even when he stood and motioned for me to move, even when he walked around the desk and asked me in a stern voice if I'd like a detention to go with my failing grade, I stayed perfectly still until he reached out his hand and gripped my arm.

His touch felt like a brand and I jerked away from him, the buzzing in my ears suddenly gone, bringing the world around me into harsh, startling clarity. The lights were too bright, the sound of the student's laughter too loud, the feel of the stale air on my skin was too fucking harsh. I needed out. If I stayed there for one more second, I'd lose it. I'd lose whatever tiny thread of control I may have once had.

I bolted.

My thought processes slowed and narrowed until the only thing I could think about was escape and the only thing I could feel was the slapping of my feet against the floor as they took me further from Mr. Ford, from my ruined paper, from a zero.

My chest seemed to tighten with every step I took until even the tiniest of breaths was painful and by the time I reached the front doors of the school, I felt like I might die if I didn't get some fresh air.

Only, when I managed to push the door open and stumble down the front steps, my lungs were still burning, my heart still hammering and my head was starting to spin.

"No," I moaned, clutching a hand to my chest, recognizing what was going on here. I felt like my heart was trying to claw its way out of my chest, like my lungs were working furiously but no oxygen was penetrating, like my brain was telling my body to function and my body was ignoring it.

I half ran, half stumbled towards my car, deliriously thinking that if I only made it there, if I could just get there, I'd be fine. The pain would disappear and I could breathe again.

I tripped when I was only a couple feet away and my shoulder slammed into the side of my vehicle, creating a new dent and landing my ass on the pavement. I barely felt it. I couldn't focus on anything past the way my chest was burning, the way my lungs were starving, the way my throat was locked up tight.

It's in your head, Nell, I tried to tell myself but it was no use. I was too far gone this time, this morning's close call having paved the way for a full blown panic attack. My hand gripped my shirt over my heart in a vain attempt to force the abused organ to work right, to stop hurting, to just let me be normal for once. My other hand lay at my side, anchoring me to the ground, my palm digging into the stones until they broke the skin of my already scraped flesh. I blinked a few times, realizing the edges of my vision were going dark, the shadows crowding in towards the centre until the only thing I could see were pinpricks of light, small glimpses of the real world that I could never really belong to, a world full of people who didn't have cabinets full of prescription drugs, who didn't have trouble breathing if their erasers weren't lined up properly.

Or got a zero on a paper.

A thought drifted through my mind briefly, one about stars and names but it was gone before it could fully form. Even the pinprick of light I could see was gone now, leaving me in darkness as I struggled for breath that wasn't coming, my body still fighting for something that my mind had given up on a while ago.

I was past the point of fighting, anyway. This panic attack had been inevitable so why not just go with it? Besides, now that my vision had gone black, I was starting to feel a bit...warm. It was weird but even though I could still feel my heart racing and hear my breathing sawing in and out of my lungs in short, painful pants, a strange warmth had begun to seep into my skin starting at my face.

This had never happened before.

Maybe this is just a whole new level of crazy.

Maybe it was crazy but just now, I didn't care. I felt the warmth in my cheeks and oddly, it had moved to my hands, too. It seeped into my skin, heating my blood and forcing the darkness to recede, loosening the muscles in my throat until I could almost take a full breath of air.

I didn't fight it. I let it happen even though a part of my mind was whispering at me that this wasn't entirely right, that it didn't work like this, that panic attacks never came with a comforting wave of heat.

Still, I leaned into it, grabbing hold of the sensation and gripping hard, pulling it towards me, needing it closer.

Then my vision cleared.

I blinked three times before I realized Grayson West was sitting right in front of me, his dark eyes almost totally black, his brow furrowed as he stared at me.

And that heat? The one that started in my cheeks?

Yeah, that was his hands. His hands were on my cheeks, cupping my face as if his grip on me would somehow stop me from completely losing my mind.

I frowned at that thought, realizing belatedly that, well, it wasn't far off the mark.

I'd felt it. I knew I was going over the edge, losing my hold on whatever reality I usually managed to maintain and then...

He brought me back.

This is ridiculous.

You couldn't just touch someone and stop a panic attack...could you?

I mean, there had to be other factors, right? I'd been practicing deep breathing, maybe that had helped. Or maybe it was——

Oh god, were my hands pressed against his chest?

They were. They so were. I could feel it. Even though I couldn't seem to tear my eyes away from his, I could feel the warmth where my palms connected with his skin, feeling the heat through his t-shirt.

I needed to pull back, to move away, maybe move to another country but...

I was stuck. Totally caught in whatever spell he'd cast to bring me back from the edge, locked in his dark gaze.

His lips were moving. He was talking to me but the buzzing in my ears was blocking the sound of his voice so I just sat there, helpless and pathetic as he kept up a steady dialogue that might as well have been in another language.

Was he mocking me? Was he going to go back to his friends later and laugh about this, realizing once and for all that I really was the crazy girl everyone made me out to be?

I wouldn't blame him if he did. I really wouldn't except...

He didn't look like he was mocking me.

In fact, he kind of looked...worried.

Was that even possible? Could Grayson West be...worried about me?

Me?

I felt the left corner of my mouth twitch at the ridiculous thought and I watched as Grayson's eyes locked on my lips before shifting back to my eyes. "...better now? For a while there I thought you couldn't even hear me. Can you hear me now?" he asked, his voice low and smooth and for some reason I had to resist the urge to close my eyes and just listen as he spoke for a while.

I nodded slightly and watched in silence as his lips tilted up in one corner. "Good," he said, his voice just a bit gruffer now as his hands slid along my cheeks until his fingers were tangled in my hair, probably ruining my bun but I couldn't find it within me to care. "You sure you're with me, Cupcake?" he asked after a moment.

I swallowed hard, clearing my throat slightly before saying, "Don't call me Cupcake."

His crooked smile widened and some of the concern in his eyes was overshadowed by amusement. "Well, that answers that question."

I blinked a few times, my breathing almost normal now as I stared at him, wondering what the hell was going on here. Slowly, I pulled my hands away from his chest, inwardly wincing at the way I'd clung to him, leaving a few spots of blood on his t-shirt.

If he didn't think I was crazy before...

He leaned back slightly, his hands sliding off my face until he wasn't touching me anymore. I looked down at my own hands, feeling like I should apologize for staining his shirt.

"What happened?" he asked, drawing my attention. He was looking at my hands, frowning but after a second, he looked up to meet my gaze and I could see that he wasn't really asking about my cuts.

He was asking about the total meltdown he'd just witnessed in our school parking lot.

"I should get cleaned up," I said hoarsely, feeling a bit like I'd just run a race, like my legs weren't quite strong enough to hold me up anymore.

Good thing I was already leaning against my car.

I started to stand, my cheeks starting to burn with embarrassment because I couldn't help but think of what that must've seemed like to him.

I must've been a hyperventilating, shaky mess when he found me. I wouldn't be surprised if I'd been frothing at the mouth.

"You can't drive like this," Grayson said, his tone hard as he watched me struggle to stand. After a couple of seconds, he made a sound low in his throat and his arm was around my waist, tugging me up until I was fully vertical.

"Thanks," I muttered, not looking at him as I turned to open my car door.

I tugged but it was jammed. I pulled harder but there was no telltale screeching of poorly oiled hinges, no ominous creaking, no movement whatsoever.

I was about to pull again when I realized that there was a large hand pressed to the doorframe, halting any progress I may have made. "What are you doing?" I asked, my voice quiet and scratchy, like I was recovering from a cold.

"I told you, Cupcake, you can't drive like this."

"I have to go," I said through gritted teeth, the school feeling like a physical presence behind me, beckoning me to go back but at the same time, pushing me away.

"Okay, where are you going? I'll give you a ride."

"No," I snapped, turning around to glare at him. "I don't wa——"

"Five minutes ago, I was trying to figure out whether or not you were dying, Nell. If you think I'm going to let you get in that car and drive away, you're seriously unhinged."

That was what would convince him I was crazy?

I continued to glare at him, neither of us moving an inch.

Finally, he sighed, shifting back slightly to remove his leather jacket. "Here," he said, wrapping the jacket around my shoulders, tugging the lapels close together over my chest. "With this and the helmet, no one will recognize you, Cupcake. You'll just be some girl on the back of my bike."

I rolled my eyes. "Every girl's fantasy," I muttered, pushing my arms into the sleeves of his jacket despite my intentions of shrugging it off.

He shot me a cocky smile. "Not everyone's as lucky as you, Cupcake."

I shook my head but didn't bother replying. I'd only succeed in inflating his ego further.

When he held out his helmet to me, I took it without hesitation, a part of me screaming at myself to stop, to go back to school, to be the Nell everyone expected me to be.

But the other part of me just wanted to get on the back of his bike.

And because I'd recently suffered from a panic attack, my brain wasn't working properly so I did the exact thing I shouldn't have.

I got onto the back of Grayson's bike.

The motorcycle started with a loud roar, the power of the engine making the whole thing thrum. "Where to?" he shouted over the sound.

"Anywhere," I shouted back.

"Works for me," he said and I could swear I heard a grin in his voice.

I didn't have time to think about it because the second I had my arms wrapped around his waist, we were gone.

For a moment, terror engulfed me and I was pretty sure I'd be having another panic attack shortly but then, it was just...gone.

I wasn't thinking about papers or grades or Mr. Ford. I wasn't even thinking about my mother and what she'd say if she saw me right now.

No, the only thing I could think about was...this.

For once, I wasn't overanalysing things. For once, I was just...right here.

And right here...it was pretty amazing.

I still felt a little beaten from the panic attack but the adrenaline coursing through my veins thanks to being on the back of Grayson's bike was going a long way towards erasing my pain.

"This is probably a bad idea," I said quietly, knowing he couldn't hear me as I leaned my helmeted head against his broad back, a part of me thinking it odd that a somewhat terrifying motorcycle ride could actually calm my nerves while the other part of me was too relaxed to care.

I let my eyes drift closed, pushing the rest of the world away as we rode.

I hope he never stops.

"Cupcake."

My forehead wrinkled and I tightened my arms around his waist, upset that he would interrupt this for me. Didn't he know I needed this?

An image flashed in my mind of his face the moment the panic attack had receded enough to focus on him.

Oh god, he saw me. He looked right at me while I'd been——

"We're getting off now, Cupcake."

I blinked my eyes open, lifting my head from his back to look around, trying to ignore the embarrassment seeping into my consciousness.

He saw me.

"Where are we?" I asked, taking in the trees and the wide, paved path leading towards a swing set and some slides.

"It's a park. We're at a park."

I narrowed my eyes at the back of his head, hearing the sarcastic tone in his voice. "Yeah, I got that. Why are we here?"

He sighed. "Listen," he said, bringing his hands to my forearms and prying them away from his waist.

Which was the moment I realized I'd still been holding onto him as if my life depended on it.

Oh my god.

I pulled my hands back, fumbling my way off the motorcycle immediately, ripping the helmet from my head and plunking it onto the seat before taking a few steps away from him and his demon bike.

How long had we been sitting there?

How long had I been clinging to him like he was my only lifeline?

"Hey," he said, dismounting from the bike before closing the distance between us. He reached his hand towards me and I frowned as it came closer, unable to comprehend what he was doing until his palm was touching my cheek. My eyes widened and I forgot how to breathe as my gaze met his, seeing some of that concern I thought I'd imagined earlier back in his expression. "You okay, Cupcake? You look kind of pale."

"Stop calling me that," I hissed, stepped back, letting his fingers slide along my skin until he was no longer touching me.

His eyes narrowed slightly and he pulled his arm down quickly, tucking his hand into the pocket of his jeans as he glared at me. "I would but I'm having too much fun pissing you off…Cupcake."

He turned his back on me and began walking towards the park, obviously unconcerned whether I followed him or not.

I stared at his broad back, irritation making my hands clench into fists which made me wince from the scrapes on my palms.

"What the hell is wrong with you?" I asked, trailing behind him, taking long strides to catch up.

"Me? You're the one who can't handle a stupid nickname," he grumbled, picking up his pace and increasing the distance between us.

I ground my teeth, letting out an odd sound in the back of my throat as my anger multiplied.

Did I just growl?

"Should I be jumping for joy then? How many times have I told you that I don't like it?"

He shrugged. "Then I'll stop."

"You will?" I asked, stumbling over my own feet slightly, shocked that he'd caved so easily. Was that all it took? Had I just needed to explai——

"Probably not," he said, shooting me a self satisfied smirk, toying with me.

I growled again.

"You're such an asshole!" I half shouted, my anger making me forget that I didn't shout, that I didn't lose control and yell at people in public parks even if we were one town over.

He stopped in his tracks, turning slowly to face me, the crooked, gloating grin on his face making a whisper of trepidation curl through my blood.

Unfortunately, I was too pissed off the pay attention to the warning signs and found myself taking a step closer to him and saying defensively, "What? You can call me whatever you want but as soon as I call you an asshole you take offense? God, for such a "tough guy" you sure are sensitive."

His grin amped up a couple notches and suddenly, he was right in front of me, his breath fanning across my lips, his chest brushing against mine. He reached out a hand and curled his fingers around the nape of my neck, tilting my head slightly to the side so he could bring his lips close to my ear. I felt my eyes widen at the contact, my breath hitching once before disappearing entirely as his touch short circuited something vital in my brain.

Move! a small, remaining piece of my mind shouted at me, begging my feet to run far, far away from him.

Unfortunately, I'd lost all motor functions the second his calloused fingers had touched my sensitive skin and that shout of dissent had sounded more like a whisper to me. A very easily ignored whisper.

"You didn't seem to think I was an asshole when you were wrapped around me on my bike a few minutes ago." My eyes got impossibly wider as his words sank in, embarrassment and rage warring for purchase in my racing head. He shifted back slightly so he could see my face, his smile smug as he eyed me down. "Cupcake," he finished succinctly, bringing his hand up to chuck me under the chin before turning his back on me and walking away, looking like he was about to whistle in contentment.

Had he just…did he seriously just…?

The rage that had previously been coursing through me multiplied and without any conscious thought, I found myself following him, my steps echoing off the pavement as the distance between us grew smaller and smaller.

I watched as my fist flung towards him, my knuckles connected with the back of one of his shoulders hard enough to make a weird thudding sound as my fist bounced off of with what felt like rock solid muscle.

I was watching myself pull my arm back to repeat the process when I realized I'd completely lost my mind.

"I am not just some girl who got on the back of your bike, Grayson. I did not wrap myself around you so don't you dare make it seem like I was…like I was trying to…" I trailed off, my fist glancing off his shoulder as he turned to face me.

"C'mon Nell, if you beat me up, who's going to drive you home?"

I pulled my hand back to punch him again. "I can't believe that you'd suggest that I…" I hissed, letting my fist fly while simultaneously wondering what the hell was wrong with me.

Before I even connected, he had my wrist in his hand and he'd tugged me forward, slamming my chest against his, my feet tripping over each other as I stumbled into him and I would've fallen on my face if his other arm hadn't wrapped around my waist, keeping me vertical.

I froze, suddenly very aware that I was plastered against Grayson West. Had he always been so tall? Had his shoulders always been that broad? And his chest——

"You can't be seen with me in public." I blinked, my brain moving a little sluggishly, trying to understand what he was talking about. "I haven't forgotten," he said, his eyes a little...flat as he stared down at me, his voice devoid of emotion even as his arm kind of tightened around me a second before letting me go. "You're not just some girl. You're Nell Watson."

He stepped away from me and turned his back, heading further along the path. I frowned after him, my steps slow as I followed, wondering why I suddenly missed hearing him call me Cupcake.

We rounded a corner and I spotted a few chess tables set up, most of them occupied by seniors, each of them immersed in the game until we walked into view.

"Grayson!" one of the old men said, grinning over at Grayson. "What are you doing here on a weekday? Couldn't wait until Saturday to get your ass kicked?"

"In your dreams, Earl. You and I both know you never beat me," Grayson replied easily, shooting the man a quick smile.

"Only because I let you win," Earl grumbled, his eyes shifting to me. "She with you?" he asked, his grin getting a little wider as he looked me up and down.

I shifted uncomfortably, my hand automatically reaching up to see if my bun was out of place, frowning slightly when I realized it was perfect.

When had I fixed it? It had to have been messy when I took the helmet off...

"This is Nell," Grayson replied, gesturing towards me before heading to a table and taking a seat.

"She's pretty," the man sitting across from Earl said, giving me a kind smile.

"She's definitely pretty. Makes me wonder what she's doing with Gray," Earl said, smirking over at Grayson before sending a softer smile in my direction.

My lips twitched slightly as I moved closer to where Grayson was sitting.

"Ignore them," he said, setting up the pieces. "Want to play?"

I shrugged, taking the seat across from him. "Sure."

"Don't worry," he said, smirking at me. "I'll go easy on you."

I rolled my eyes. "You do that."

It took longer than I'd expected and there were times I'd wondered if I'd even pull it off, but eventually, I won.

"Checkmate," I said, trying not to sound too smug.

"No way," Grayson said, staring down at the board in bewilderment.

"Well done, girlie," Earl said, slapping me on the back as he grinned widely. "Finally, someone who can beat him."

Grayson's eyes narrowed on Earl then swung to me. "Best two out of three."

I shrugged and reached to replace the pieces to their starting position.

The second game took even longer and I wasn't entirely surprised when Grayson moved his rook before crossing his arms over his chest and saying, "Checkmate."

"Last game," I muttered, shifting the pieces back to their original position, resolving to win this one. He was good, but I was just getting started. It had been a long time since I'd played and the first two games were just warm ups.

He was going down.

"You can't let him win, Nellie. He gloats. He'll never let it go," Earl said close to my ear, wrinkling his nose in Grayson's direction before going back to his own game.

I smothered a laugh, clearing my throat when Grayson quirked a brow in my direction. "Your move," I said.

He shifted his pawn forward. "So, what happened today?"

My hand froze in midair, my fingers almost touching my knight. "What do you mean?" I asked, playing dumb, hoping that he wasn't talking about what he was probably talking about.

"In the parking lot, at school. Was that a panic attack?" he asked, moving his piece once I'd finally managed to place mine.

I shifted uncomfortably on the bench. "Yeah."

"What causes them?" he asked, lifting his gaze to meet mine, his expression unreadable.

I shrugged, trying to play it cool when really, my stomach was rolling uncomfortably, my mind was racing, trying to come up with excuses, anything but the truth, and my heart was beating a hole in my chest. "I...got a zero on a paper," I said softly, my voice sounding weak to my own ears.

Why couldn't I just shrug and pretend like it was no big deal? So I had a panic attack. Big deal. People got them all the time.

Only...

He saw me.

I looked down at the board, inwardly wincing at the thought. "I know it sounds stupid."

"Maybe there was more than one trigger," he said, reaching out to gently lift one of my hands, turning it so that my palm was facing upwards, exposing the poorly bandaged skin there.

I pulled my hand away, putting it on my lap. "Maybe," I replied.

Drop it, Grayson.

"I thought you were dying," he said after a minute, his eyes getting a little darker as he looked at me.

"It feels like it," I whispered, wondering why I was telling him any of this.

A muscle in his jaw ticked and he clenched and unclenched his hand before shifting his next piece. "How do you stop it?" His voice was a bit lower now, a bit gruffer as he eyed the game critically, looking completely engulfed.

Except, there was a tension in his shoulders that chess didn't warrant and that muscle in his jaw hadn't stopped ticking. It was almost like he was waiting for my answer. Like it was important.

"I don't know. Time, I guess." Or you, apparently, I added silently, watching him through my lashes, thinking about how it had felt this time and remembering that heat that had started in my cheeks, feeling it warm me from the inside out.

"What causes them?" he asked, still not meeting my eyes.

"Loose screws," I mumbled, wishing he'd let this go.

"I'm serious," he said, his intense gaze lifting to meet my eyes.

I blinked at his severe expression. "This isn't your problem, Grayson."

"What if it happens again?" he ground out, the fingers on his right hand curling into a fist as he narrowed his eyes at me. "I want to know what to do. I don't want to just sit there like an idiot the way I did today."

"It won't happen again," I hedged, my voice weak.

"You don't know that," he snapped.

I sighed, sitting back slightly, my feet itching to run away from this uncomfortable conversation. "You don't have to worry about it, Grayson."

"Just tell me what causes them."

I sighed, shrugging my shoulders and giving in. "Stress, mostly. Sometimes if I'm really tired it takes less to...send me over the edge." I shut my mouth to keep from elaborating. There was no way I'd be telling him just how little it took to 'send me over the edge'. Failing a paper was one thing but I'd had a panic attack before because my hair elastic broke.

He already thinks you're crazy. No need to give him more ammo.

"Weren't you going to stop caring?" he said, his low tone making me blink before my eyes locked on his.

I frowned. "About school?"

He shook his head. "About what they think, Nell."

I lost my breath at the way he was looking at me, like he wanted to reach out and grab my shoulders and shake me until I saw reason but also...

It also kind of seemed like he wanted to…protect me.

Ridiculous.

I shook my head, giving what I hoped was a casual shrug and a careless smile as I said, "Easier said than done."

His forehead wrinkled and he clenched his jaw, but before he could say anything, a man walked up to our table and planted his hands on the edge. "Hey, West." I glanced over at the newcomer who shot me a wide smile before focusing on Grayson. "Shouldn't you be in school?"

Grayson's expression darkened and he was clenching his jaw so hard that I thought I heard his teeth grind together. "What the hell are you doing here, Dex?"

"Looking for you. Your brother said I might find you here. Guess he was right," Dex said, picking up a pawn and tossing it into the air before catching it again, repeating the process as he focused on me. He was thin and not much older than us but there was something about the way he stood, the way he casually tossed the chess piece in the air that made me think that he was anything but weak. His eyes were a light hazel colour and his face was handsome enough or at least it would be if he wasn't look at me like a wolf looks at its prey. "Who's this?"

"Go away," Grayson growled, his black eyes projecting a warning that the other boy was not paying attention to.

"Relax, man. I just came to invite you to a little get together," Dex sighed, putting the pawn back on the table. "As you know, your brother got out a couple days ago. He wants to see you. We're having a little celebration tomorrow night at my place. You should be there, Gray." Dex's eyes slid over to me and he gave me a once over, a hint of disdain entering his expression. "Bring your girl if you want but I think one of our parties might be a bit much for her."

"Come on," Grayson said suddenly standing. He was obviously talking to me but he never took his eyes off of Dex. "We're leaving."

I stood but I must not have moved fast enough for Grayson because suddenly he was gripping my wrist, propelling me along the path behind him.

"I'll see you there, Gray!" Dex shouted after us just before we turned a corner, moving out of sight.

As soon as Dex could no longer see us, Grayson dropped my wrist and lengthened his stride. I frowned, practically having to jog to keep up.

He stopped next to his bike, his hands clenched into fists as he stared into the parking lot, fury radiating off of him in waves.

"Fuck," he snarled, turning his back on his bike so he could pace a few feet away, his strides stiff as he turned and paced back, running a hand through his hair.

"Grayson," I said, standing next to his motorcycle, watching him pace and feeling completely useless.

"I just need a minute," he said through gritted teeth, continuing to pace.

I nodded, letting him go for awhile but the more he paced, the more pissed off he seemed to be getting and before I could really think about what I was doing, I was walking towards him. He didn't seem to notice me and was turning his back when I suddenly reached out and gripped his hand in mine.

He stopped as if he'd hit a wall, his back going ramrod straight as soon as my fingers tightened around his palm.

What am I doing?

I blinked down at our hands before lifting my gaze to his stiff back, my eyes following the lines of his shoulder blades, seeing the tension in his neck and the way his dark hair stood on end from his hands running through it repeatedly.

"Grayson," I said, my voice quiet but strong as I shifted slightly so that I could see his face. His eyes were turbulent, his expression dark and taut as he stared down at me like I was an alien being. I didn't let go of his hand. "Are you okay?"

He didn't blink. His expression didn't change. He just kept staring down at me, not even moving as I stood there like a lunatic, holding his hand and asking Grayson West, local badass, if he was okay.

"Talk to me," I said softly, my forehead wrinkling with worry when he still didn't reply. Who the hell was that guy and why would he have the power to rattle Grayson this way?

I took a step closer to him, tilting my head back a little further so I could still meet his eyes. "Grayson?"

His brow furrowed but some of the tension eased from his shoulders as his gaze shifted to our hands. At some point, his hand had tightened around mine, his callused palm engulfing my scratched one. "I can't figure you out, Nell Watson," he said, his voice rumbling from his chest.

He couldn't figure me out?

There were about a million questions swirling in my head after that little encounter, none of which I felt like I could ask.

I didn't know what to say to that, so I just stood there, taking him in as he kept his gaze locked on our hands. My eyes drifted over his thick, dark hair, liking how it stood up at every possible angle, defying gravity without the help of any styling gel, liking that he didn't feel the need to smooth it out.

"Let's go," he finally said, looking up to meet my eyes again, giving me a look I couldn't quite decipher, like he was asking me a question but I didn't know what it was.

I nodded and after a pause, he moved towards his bike, keeping his hold on my hand until he had to let it go to pick up the spare helmet and pass it to me.

Grayson's POV

I'm in serious trouble here.

My heart was beating so hard it felt like it might rip a hole through my chest while we drove around, heading nowhere.

Part of why we had no destination was because I literally couldn't think at the moment.

Every time I managed to focus on something, it had to do with the girl sitting behind me with her arms wrapped around my waist and her helmeted head resting on my back like it was the most natural thing in the world.

And thinking about Nell Watson right now was not an option.

Because the second I started thinking about her, I would remember the way she'd wrinkled her brow, thinking about her next move in chess, the way she'd tried to tuck away her smug smile when she won.

The way she'd taken my hand when I felt like I was about to explode.

Which was the most dangerous thought running through my head because as soon as I thought that, I'd remember exactly what it felt like when she'd touched me, her smaller hand gripping mine gently but somehow it had felt like I'd been hit by a freight train.

Didn't she know? Hadn't she heard? People didn't just walk up to me and hold my hand. People didn't look at me with concern in their eyes and ask me if I was okay.

Most people, as in everyone else who was not Nell Watson, would've given me a wide berth at that moment. Most people would've moved further away, possibly crossed a street to put some distance between us.

Then there was Nell.

She's not afraid of me.

I don't know why that surprised me. Of all the times I'd pissed her off and all the times she'd managed to do the same to me, I couldn't think of a single instance when there had been fear in her pretty silver eyes.

Even when she'd been having her panic attack, which was not something I'd like to see again, she'd reached for me, like I was somehow holding her together.

It's because she doesn't talk to the people at school. She hasn't heard the rumours. She doesn't know.

I sighed, giving my head a mental shake as we turned into the school's parking lot.

Hadn't I planned on not thinking about her?

I pulled in a parking spot and cut the engine, oddly disappointed when she immediately dismounted, leaving my back feeling cold.

I got off the bike, not really sure where we stood anymore. She couldn't be seen with me in public but she wasn't afraid to grab my hand when I was about to lose my shit. She could piss me off with just one look but the past week of pretending that she didn't exist had been almost impossible. My eyes were drawn to her. I'd see her walking down the hallway with her head down, her brow creased in thought and I'd want to go to her, to call her Cupcake, to see her silver eyes go molten the way they did when I pissed her off.

But she'd made it pretty clear that we weren't friends and we never could be.

My left hand fisted at the thought, not liking the idea of going back to ignoring her after today.

"I should go get my stuff," she said, jerking a thumb over her shoulder towards the school. I stood from my bike and she placed the spare helmet on the seat I'd just vacated. She wasn't meeting my eyes.

Her phone must've gone off in her pocket because she jumped slightly, frowning as she retrieved it and looked at the screen.

"Your boyfriend?" I asked, my voice coming out lower than I'd intended, less teasing and more...menacing thanks to the name I'd seen flash across the screen.

"Craig's not my boyfriend," she said, putting the phone back in her pocket without answering his text.

I snorted, remembering the way the guy had practically been glued to her at his stupid party. "Yeah, you might want to tell him that."

"We're friends," she snapped, glaring at me.

I nodded, gritting my teeth at the implied part of what she was saying; that the two of us were not.

"Whatever you say, Cupcake."

She sighed and brought a hand up to push any stray strands of hair back into her bun only when she touched her head, she realized that the whole thing was a mess, that the hair elastic was barely hanging on and there were loose strands of wispy locks all over the place, framing her face and brushing the skin on her neck.

I shoved my hands into my pockets to stop myself from reaching for her.

Then she went ahead and took the elastic out of her hair completely, letting the strands fall over her shoulders and down her back in loose waves. I swallowed hard, telling myself it would be a very bad idea to close the distance between us right now, that I was just confused because she didn't run away from me earlier, that I just needed some time to remember that I was not attracted to Nell Watson and even if I was, I'd be the last person on earth she would want touching her.

"The bell's going to ring any second now," she said, tilting her head to the side as she looked up at me, like she was trying to figure me out. "Thank you for today," she said after a long pause, her voice soft and sincere.

"Anytime," I replied, meaning it. I seriously needed to get my head on straight when it came to this girl.

Not that it mattered anyway. The odds of her ever talking to me again after today were slim to none.

With that, she turned her back, walking towards the school.

I gritted my teeth, turning to face my bike so I wouldn't have to watch her walk away from me. Something about seeing her retreating form really wasn't sitting well with me.

Not good, West. This is not good.

I put the spare helmet back in its compartment and was about to climb onto the bike when I felt her hand wrap around my wrist.

My stomach dropped and my heart sped up as soon as I felt her skin on mine.

"Your jacket," she said, holding it out to me as I turned to face her.

Something like disappointment curled in my gut as I took it from her, having forgotten she was even wearing it. "Thanks."

She nodded and when I expected her to move away, to walk out of my life and never come back, she shot me a grin instead.

I felt an answering smile on my lips almost immediately but I squashed it before it could fully form. There was no reason for her to know that her smiles made something in my brain short circuit and if she caught me grinning like a moron just because she happened to smile in my near vicinity, it would kind of be a dead giveaway.

"Don't think you're off the hook, Grayson." I frowned trying to focus past that grin of hers and the humour sparkling in her eyes. Had anyone else ever seen her like this? With her hair down and a smile on her face...she was beautiful.

"What?" I asked, feeling like my brain was working twice as hard just to form coherent thoughts.

"The game. You owe me a tiebreaker and I'm not going easy on you next time."

The smile I'd been struggling against worked its way past my defenses and I found myself leaning a little closer to her as I said, "You'd better start practicing, Cupcake because there isn't a chance in hell you're going to win."

She shrugged, looking unconcerned. "We'll see."

Chapter 7

Nell's POV

"Don't be mad at me," Craig said, sinking into his chair and twisting so that he was facing me.

I quirked a brow, my eyes darting to the stack of books he'd carelessly plopped onto the desk. My fingers itched to straighten them, to make sure all the spines were facing the same direction and all the edges were lined up. "Why would I be mad at you?" I asked, distracted.

"I told my dad you were looking for a job."

My gaze shot to his, my eyes going wide as his words sank in. "Why?"

"He's partner at his law firm. I figured he might be able to find something for you." Craig scanned my face, looking for clues to determine what I was thinking. "It would look good on your college application?" he said, uncertain.

I frowned. "He doesn't even know me. I've never even met him." I shook my head. "Why would he want to hire me?"

"It's not guaranteed, Nell. You'd still have to give him your resume and go for an interview. I just mentioned that you were looking for work and he said to send you to him. He wants to meet you."

I blinked, narrowing my eyes at him. "He does? How does he even know who I am?"

He shrugged, looking down at the scarred desk in front of him, his long, athletic fingers reaching out to flip through his chemistry textbook aimlessly. "Your name's come up in conversation a few times."

"You talk about me with your parents?" I mumbled, shocked.

His gaze locked on mine, something like determination filtering into his features. "We're friends," he said, his lips tilting into a warm smile as he gave his shoulders a slight shrug. Clearing his throat, he continued. "Is it so weird that I mention you from time to time?" His lips tilted a little further. "Are you saying you never talk about me with your folks?"

My spine straightened and something cold slithered through my veins. "They're not much for idle chit-chat." Understatement. They could barely stand it when I talked about myself, never mind bringing another person into the conversation.

In fact, I think they might even prefer it when I didn't talk at all.

Facing forward, I took my pens from their case and lined them up at the top of my desk, barely stopping myself from getting out a ruler to make sure they were all the same distance apart.

"Nell," Craig said, his voice quiet, gentle as he reached out and placed his hand on top of mine, staying my movements. When I looked over at him, that determination was back in his eyes and when he swallowed hard, I frowned. Was he nervous about something? "The truth is——"

"Hope I'm not interrupting anything," Grayson said, pulling a stool up to the shared desk where Craig and I were sitting. He sank onto the stool, eyeing Craig's hand still resting on top of mine.

I pulled my hand away, breaking the contact.

"What do you want, West?" Craig snapped, his tone bordering on hostile.

"I had a question about the homework. I was hoping Cupcake could enlighten me."

"What is it?" I asked, not even bothering to remind him not to call me that.

"Number four," he said, opening his notebook and shifting the stool so that he was closer to me, our bent heads nearly touching.

I frowned down at his work, seeing that he'd gotten all the other questions with no issues. "This question is really similar to number three and you got that one. Which part has you stumped?"

"All of it," he said vaguely, resting his hand next to my pens, shifting them one by one until they sat at an angle.

My teeth gritted and I barely resisted the urge to straighten them. "Okay, I'll walk you through it."

One of Craig's friends had shown up and started talking to him but I could feel his gaze on me every once in a while, his disapproval obvious.

Once I was finished the question, I looked up to find Grayson already looking at me. "Get it?" I asked, wondering if he'd even been paying attention.

"Yeah," he said, one corner of his lips tilted up in a crooked grin. "So, I was thinking about that paper you wrote and the more I think about it, the more it pisses me off."

I shrugged, inwardly wincing at the reminder of my failing grade. "I'll do some extra credit."

"You shouldn't have to," he said, his grin fading, his dark eyes getting a little darker.

"I don't have much of a choice."

"Want me to beat him up?"

My lips twitched but I shook my head. "No, thanks."

"You sure?"

I felt a smile slip onto my lips, pretending to consider it for a moment before giving a resigned sigh. "I'm positive."

He blinked a couple times, his gaze going a little unfocused for a second, like he was distracted by something. "Nell——"

"Mr. West, is there any chance you'll be taking your own seat sometime today?" Mr. Wright snapped, arms crossed as he glared at the back of Grayson's head.

"Only if you say please," Grayson replied, turning slightly so he could shoot Mr. Wright a mocking grin.

"Get to your seat or you'll be in detention all next week."

Grayson sighed and stood, grabbing his notebook from my desk as he gave a salute to the teacher. Leaning close to my ear, he whispered, "Thanks, Cupcake," before heading towards his own desk, propping his feet up and leaning back in his chair as soon as Mr. Wright began the lecture.

"What was that about?" Craig whispered, leaning in close. "Since when are you friends with Grayson West?"

I blinked, my eyes falling on the pens that were still sitting at an angle. "He's been...decent to me," I said, reaching out to straighten my pens. "I'm returning the favour."

From the corner of my eye, I saw Craig's hand clench into a fist before it relaxed again. "Just be careful. He's not the type of person you can trust, Nell."

I nodded, focusing on Mr. Wright, intent on listening to what he was telling us about the experiment we'd be doing that day.

But my attention was divided. Craig's words kept whispering in my head. He's not the type of person you can trust, Nell.

The odd thing was...I did trust him. Why else would I get on his bike with him? Why else would I have reached for him when I was having a panic attack?

Despite Grayson's reputation, somewhere deep down inside of me, beneath all of the insecurities and fears, some gut feeling was telling me to trust him.

When Mr. Wright finished with the instructions, Craig and I did the experiment, the two of us used to working together. Because I was a control freak, I did all the measuring, making sure everything was exact. Craig poured the concoctions and jotted down the data.

"There's a game right after school, do you mind if I leave early?" Craig said, just as we were finishing the experiment.

I shook my head, giving him a reassuring smile, a part of me glad that he'd be leaving me alone for the clean-up. I preferred doing it myself, anyway.

"Thanks, Nell," he said, shooting me a grin as he took off his apron and goggles.

He collected his books and turned to leave but stopped suddenly, turning back towards me, his blue eyes unreadable. "Nell, I..." he trailed off, his forehead wrinkling as he seemed to search for the right words but with a wave of his hand, decided to let it go. "Never mind. I'll see you tomorrow."

I frowned, staring after him as he left, wondering what the heck was going on with him.

Shaking my head, I stood, washing the beakers thoroughly before drying them. I brought the beakers to their shelf and placed them inside, adjusting the rest of them so that the spouts were all at one o'clock. Satisfied, I closed the door and stepped back, directly into a hard object.

I jumped and spun, my eyes narrowing when they landed on Grayson. "What's your problem?" I snapped, stepping around him to get back to my desk.

"I'm not the one running into people, Cupcake," he said, resting a hip against Craig's half of the table.

"You snuck up on me," I grumbled, gathering my books, belatedly noticing that the rest of the class had already left for the day.

"You were too absorbed in perfectly aligning all the beakers to notice that I was there." He planted a hand on his chest and gave me a mockingly sorrowful look. "It hurts me to think that you care more about those beakers than you do about me, Cupcake."

"I can't help it if they're more interesting," I blurted, my eyes going wide as soon as the words left my mouth.

He stared at me for a long beat before tilting his head back and giving a deep chuckle.

Oh.

Everything inside of me went still as I watched his lips stretch, watched his throat work. Had people called him dangerous? Because right now, with that deep laugh echoing in my ears, I just couldn't see it.

In fact, at this moment, Grayson West was undeniably...

Attractive.

I sucked in a quick breath of air, giving myself a mental shake as I took a step away from him.

No. No way. I did not just think that. I hadn't slept well the night before and my mind was playing tricks on me. There was no way I found Grayson West attractive.

No way.

I packed up the rest of my books quickly, grabbing my bag and heading towards the door.

"Wait," he said, his hand wrapping around my wrist, halting me in my tracks.

"What?" I asked, my voice cold, distant.

He didn't let me go as he shifted, moving until he was in front of me, looking down at me with furrowed brows and something like concern in his dark gaze. "I wanted to ask you, are you okay? Yesterday with the whole...panic attack thing, I just wanted to make sure that you were," he waved his free hand in the air, searching for the words, "better, I guess."

"I'm fine," I ground out, biting my lip as I looked down at where his hand was wrapped around my wrist, willing him to let me go. It was bad enough that he'd witnessed me freaking out, was it too much to ask that he forget it ever happened?

"Good," he said, his voice a little lower as he slowly let me go before lifting his hand to run it through his hair.

I followed the movement, noticing for the first time, a tension around his shoulders that wasn't usually there. And were those bags under his eyes?

"I'd better get going," he said, giving me a nod before turning his back on me and walking out of the classroom.

Without thinking, I followed him, my hand reaching out of its own accord until my fingers were wrapped around his wrist. When he turned to face me, I swallowed hard, calling myself stupid in a thousand different ways, wondering why I was holding him back even as I refused to let him go. "Is something wrong?" I blurted, thinking back to the day before when we were playing chess when that guy came up to us. "You look kind of…" I trailed off, shaking my head, not entirely sure where I was going with this. "Are you okay?"

Slowly, he turned towards me, his eyes focused on my fingers wrapped around his wrist. We were standing just outside of the chemistry classroom now and a few students were lingering in the hallway. A part of me knew I shouldn't be doing this, I shouldn't be stopping him, I shouldn't be touching him.

I didn't let him go.

"I'm fine," he said, his voice a little lower than usual, gruffer.

I frowned, wishing he'd look at me. "Are you sure?"

A grin tipped the corners of his mouth and his gaze finally connected with mine. "You worried about me, Cupcake?" He took a step closer to me and I blinked, loosening my hold on his wrist.

"No," I blurted, retreating a step but I barely moved before my back connected with a locker.

He tilted a brow, his dark eyes sparking with teasing light as he came even closer to me, resting a hand on the locker behind me, caging me in. "You sure about that?"

"Positive," I said with a firm nod.

His lips tipped up in the corners but there was no humour in his eyes when he spoke. "It does sound weird, doesn't it? Nell Watson worried about Grayson West. Who would believe that?"

I frowned. Was it so far fetched? Was it so impossible to believe that I could worry about something other than my grades? I wasn't a robot. He looked distracted and tired so I'd asked him what was wrong. Why should that seem so foreign to him?

Maybe because you've told him you can't be seen in public with him.

I swallowed, the thought ringing clearly in my head. For someone I couldn't be seen socializing with, he sure was standing close to me.

Very close.

A shadow flickered across his eyes but in a blink it was gone, replaced by a bland look and a careless grin. "Since we've established that you're not worried for my well-being, I'm going to leave." He quirked a brow. "Unless you wanted to go for a ride somewhere?"

I blinked, shaking my head slowly, tamping down my sudden urge to go with him, to get on the back of his bike and forget everything else for a while.

"Didn't think so," he said with a firm nod and I felt something tug at the back of my head before he stepped away from me. He grinned when my hair fell around my shoulders, loosened from its usual low bun by his nimble fingers. "I'll see you around, Cupcake," he said before turning on his heel and walking away from me.

My fingers itched to fix my hair but something was holding me still, some force was keeping me exactly where I was, staring at Grayson's back as he walked away from me, his shoulders still tense, his spine still stiff no matter how carefree he acted.

I shook my head when I realized I'd unconsciously taken a couple steps in his direction.

What was the plan, Nell? Catch up to him and…pat him on the back?

Right, it was perfectly obvious how absurd he found the idea of me being worried about him. What would he say if he knew I had the insane urge to figure out what was wrong and find a way to fix it?

I gritted my teeth to hold in a derisive snort at the thought, my feet carrying me back into the classroom to see if I forgot anything.

Frowning, I pushed my stool a little further under the desk, making sure it was right in the middle and that the legs were positioned so that two were under and two out.

A wry smile twisted my lips as I brushed my hand over the seat, satisfied with the result even as a bone deep sense of sadness washed over me.

I couldn't fix Grayson's problems if I tried. I was a second away from busting out a ruler to make sure I'd positioned the stool just right. The idea that I could help Grayson in any way was laughable.

Yesterday the lines had gotten a little blurred but nothing had changed. I was still Nell Watson and he was still Grayson West.

Reaching up, I tucked my hair back into its familiar bun before leaving the chemistry room.

I'd been tossing and turning for a couple of hours when the phone rang. I picked it up, seeing Paige's name on the screen before I hastily answered. "Paige? What's wrong?"

"Can you come pick me up?" she asked, her voice small, afraid.

"Where are you?" I breathed, lurching off my bed to find some clothes.

She rattled off an address, her voice shaking slightly. My gut clenched in fear for her.

"Is Brian with you?"

"I don't know where he went," she whispered.

"I'll be there soon," I said, hanging up so I could get dressed more quickly.

In seconds, I was out of the house and in my car, driving like a maniac to get to her. My heart was racing and panic was eating at me. The address she gave me was not familiar and the closer I got, it became more obvious why.

This wasn't the bad part of town. This wasn't even close to the bad part of town. This was the part of town that people who lived in the bad part of town wouldn't even step foot in. My heart tripped in my chest thinking that Paige was here somewhere, alone.

I didn't need the address to find the party. The house was overloaded with people, men and women spilling onto the lawn, not caring that it was past midnight and they were making enough noise to wake up the entire city.

The house was big enough but looked like it could fall over with one stiff gust of wind. The siding was decaying, the paint a mere memory and the windows were dirty, caked with what looked like decades of dust.

I parked the car across the street, my chest tight as I opened my door and stepped out.

What the hell was she thinking?

This wasn't her kind of party. I didn't care how different she was now, Paige did not belong here.

I searched the crowd on the lawn as I walked towards the house but she was nowhere. A few people gave me curious looks but I moved quickly enough that no one really paid me any close attention. The smell of drugs and alcohol, sweat and sex reached me before I even got to the front door. It was open so I walked right in, a fine sheen of perspiration dotting my skin as I eyed the crush of people inside.

I needed to breathe but the air was so choked with smoke that the idea seemed unlikely. My eyes shifted over the crowd, wincing when I saw the coffee table covered with lines of white powder, glad that my sister wasn't one of the women bent over, inhaling through their noses.

These weren't high school kids. Most of these people looked to be in their mid twenties or older and none of them looked nearly as out of place as I felt.

I was about to take a step in when a fight broke out right in front of me. Two big, burly guys suddenly lunged at each other, fists swinging madly. Someone in front of me was shoved into me and I stumbled slightly, my back landing against another person with a soft thud. The person behind me wrapped his arms around my waist, steadying me while we moved further away from the fight.

I breathed a sigh of relief when it ended, people stepping in to pull the two guys apart. I turned towards the guy I'd run into and my voice caught in my throat at the sight of him. He wasn't much taller than me but he seemed to be made entirely of muscle. He was wearing a tight white t-shirt that displayed his arms which were liberally covered in tattoos, some looking more professionally done than others. His face was hard, unyielding and there was a long jagged scar along one of his cheeks.

He gave me a slow smile, licking his lips as he looked me up and down. "Where did you come from, Angel?"

"I'm looking for my sister," I croaked, not liking the way his brown eyes darkened when they rested on my chest.

"If she looks like you, she ain't here. I would've definitely noticed her." He took a step closer to me and I fought not to retreat, thinking it would be a bad idea to show this guy how scared I was at the moment.

"I'm just going to call her," I mumbled, pulling out my phone and dialling Paige's number with shaking fingers. I turned slightly away from the guy as it rang, desperate for her to answer.

It rang six times before she finally picked up. "Hello," she said, laughter in her voice and in the background.

"Paige? I'm here. Where are you?"

Her giggle was high pitched and filled with glee. "She's actually there," she said, her voice a little muffled, like she'd covered the microphone but hadn't quite covered it all the way. "Oh Nell," she said, her voice clear again. "You actually thought I'd call you?"

I blinked a few times, a weight settling on my chest as her question registered. "You're not here, are you?"

"Nope," she said, giggling again for good measure. "Brian and I stopped in earlier but realized it was a bit too heavy for us."

Betrayal hit me like a semi, making my knees shake with the force of it. "I have to go," I said, a chill settling into my limbs, working its way to my torso before reaching my heart.

"Oh come on, Nell. You have to admit it's funny! I'm picturing you in that house with all those druggies and dealers. Get someone to take a pic okay? I totally want to frame——"

I hung up before she could finish, the ice in my veins somehow making the smoke in the room seem a little less oppressive.

A hand on my wrist stopped me when I turned towards the door, intent on getting out of there now.

"Where you going, Angel? I can help you find your sister."

I turned towards the man I'd bumped into, trying to work some kind of smile onto my lips and failing. "She's not here. I'm sorry I ran into you."

He grinned at me, tugging me a little closer. "I'm not. If you don't have to find your sister then you can stay with me, can't you? Let me get you a drink, Angel."

"No, thanks," I said, trying not to let the fear show in my voice as I pulled lightly on my hand, needing him to let go of my wrist. My breathing was speeding up, my heart tripping in my chest and I still couldn't free myself of his hold. "Please let me go," I whispered. I don't think he heard me but he shook his head anyway, still grinning at me in a feral way.

The muscles in his arm bunched and I'm pretty sure he was about to tug me closer to him again when suddenly, someone else was gripping his wrist.

Jumping slightly, I turned to see Grayson standing next to me, his dark eyes on the guy still holding me. "Let her go, Vin."

Vin chuckled, tightening his grip on my wrist until it was painful. "I don't see your name on her, Gray."

"I'm not asking again," Grayson said, his eyes black, his face completely calm as he stared the other man down until something like fear flickered in Vin's eyes.

"Yeah," Vin said, unwrapping his fingers from my wrist, not taking his eyes off Grayson. "Okay." Finally, he looked at me and winked. "See you around, Angel."

"Grayson, what——"

"Shut up," he growled, taking my wrist in his hand in order to drag me out of the house and across the street. "What the fuck were you doing in there, Nell? Why the hell would you even be here?"

"Paige called me and——"

"So you came running in on your white knight?" he shouted, getting right in my face. "What the fuck were you thinking? Did you even glance at the house before you walked in there?"

"Stop yelling at me," I snapped, tugging on my wrist, trying to break his hold but he wouldn't let go. "She sounded freaked and yeah, I looked at the house but all I could think was that she was in there alone and I..." I trailed off, waving a hand in the direction of the party. "I didn't want to go in but I didn't exactly have a choice."

"You had a goddamn choice, Nell. You could've chosen to let your idiot sister deal with her own fucking problems for once!" he snarled, finally breaking his hold on my wrist so he could run a hand through his hair and pace in front of my car.

"I couldn't just leave her!" I said, my voice going a little shrill as I pushed away from my car and stepped into his path. "I'm not wired like that, okay? She sounded scared and desperate and yeah, maybe it was dumb, but I tried to help her."

He snorted, taking a step closer to me until we were nearly nose to nose. "You can't help her, Nell. If your sister is coming to a party like this one, she doesn't need a ride home, she needs an intervention."

My indignation faded and my gaze slid to the side. "Yeah well, the good news is she wasn't there."

His forehead wrinkled and his jaw clenched, setting off a muscle in his cheek. "What?"

I sighed, taking a step back and running a hand through my hair, realizing belatedly that I hadn't tied it back earlier. "It was a prank. She was messing with me and I was dumb enough to believe her." I winced at my own stupidity, hating that she could get to me so easily. When was the last time Paige had called me herself? It was always Craig or someone else at the party but never Paige. I closed my eyes and shook my head. "I'm an idiot."

"Please tell me you're joking," he said and my eyes snapped open at the tone of his voice. He was speaking slowly, like he was having trouble getting the words out but each word was laced with so much underlying rage that I felt it slip across my skin.

I frowned, a part of me wondering why I wasn't running in the other direction right now. He sounded like he was ready to lose his shit and being that I was the closest person to him, things weren't looking too bright for me.

Then again, I couldn't seem to muster the required fear when it came to Grayson West. Logically, I knew he was considered dangerous. I'd seen him beat someone up in the past and Vin with all his muscles had backed off when Grayson showed up.

Still...I wasn't scared of him.

Which was good because his tag was sticking out of his shirt and I needed to tell him to fix it before it drove me insane.

"Gray!"

We both blinked at each other before turning to look at the new guy joining us. I realized immediately that this must be Grayson's brother. They looked alike, with similar dark hair and eyes but his brother was a bit shorter and stockier. He also had tattoos almost entirely covering both his arms. I briefly wondered if Grayson had any tattoos that weren't revealed by the black t-shirt and jeans he was wearing.

"Is this your girl?" he said, looking me up and down as he came closer to us. "Not your usual type, is she?" he chuckled before sticking his hand out for me to shake. "I'm Pierce."

"Fuck off," Grayson said, smacking his brother's hand down before I even moved to grip it.

Pierce just laughed, stuffing his hands into his pockets before eyeing me again, this time with more interest in his dark eyes. "Touchy, isn't he?"

Unease slithered in my veins as Pierce continued to stare at me and I barely stopped myself from shifting closer to Grayson.

"Go back inside," Grayson snarled.

Pierce's smile vanished and his lip curled as he stared at his younger brother. "This is my getting out of jail party, Gray. I've been taking orders every single day for the past year. Don't think I'll be taking any from you."

"Then maybe I can help you along," Grayson replied, his tone filled with menace as he stepped closer to Pierce.

"Jeez," Pierce said, holding his hands up in surrender as he took a step back. "Forget it. You used to be fun, man. We used to be a team. Or did you forget about that? Too busy walking the straight and narrow to remember your own brother." He shook his head before his eyes slid back to me. "You can come back inside with me if you want, sweetheart. I'll protect you."

Grayson made a noise that sounded like a growl.

"I'll pass," I said, almost surprised when my voice came out steady.

Pierce shrugged and turned his back to us, walking towards the house. "The offer stands," he said over his shoulder, raising his hand in a wave. "See you soon, Brother."

Once his brother was inside, Grayson let out a groan and moved towards my car, resting his back against the passenger side door before cradling his face in his hands. Slowly, I moved towards him, keeping a couple feet between us as I leaned my weight onto the vehicle too.

"You should've never come here, Nell," he said, his voice muffled.

"I couldn't just leave her." My voice was soft, just above a whisper and filled with the heartache I couldn't help feeling. "She called me. She never calls me, Grayson." I shook my head and gave a mirthless laugh. "I should've known, huh?"

He let his hand fall from his face before turning towards me. "Give me your phone," he said abruptly.

I blinked but did as he asked, thinking he had to make a phone call. He pressed a few buttons before handing it back to me.

"Next time someone tells you to go pick her up, call me. I'll go with you."

I stiffened, frowning down at the phone in my hand. "I don't need your help, Grayson. She's my sister. I can handle her."

"Maybe, but if she sends you blindly into a place like this again, I want to know. Just promise me you'll call." I looked up and our eyes locked, his dark and filled with determination.

I was going to say no. I had every intention of saying no, of deleting his number from my phone and forgetting he ever asked.

But there was something in the way he was looking at me, something that had me pausing to consider his offer. If he hadn't been there tonight, I might still be trying to extract myself from Vin. More likely, I would be in there having a panic attack while a bunch of stoners watched.

"Okay," I conceded. "I'll call."

He gave a satisfied nod before shifting his gaze to the house, the party still raging hard enough for the ground beneath my feet to be vibrating.

His lips tightened and his forehead wrinkled as he looked at the building. His eyes were twin pools of obsidian and his features were set in stone. The muscles in his forearms jumped from how hard he was clenching his fists and I was pretty sure I could hear his teeth grinding.

"Is this why you were tense today? You were worried about this party?"

His gaze shot to mine and his frown deepened but he didn't respond.

"Why'd you come if you hate it so much?" I prodded, embracing the fact that I had no filter around him.

"I don't know," he finally said, his voice hoarse. "I guess I felt like I had to."

I nodded, understanding what it meant to feel obligated to your family, regardless of whether or not you wanted to be.

We were quiet for a second and I unconsciously moved a little closer to him, feeling the chill of the night air on my exposed skin. I'd only managed to throw a t-shirt on before leaving the house.

"Nell?" Grayson rasped, his face suddenly a lot closer to mine. "What are you doing?"

I blinked, my body freezing in place just as my fingers gripped the tag at the back of his shirt. I had to stand on tiptoe to reach it and without realizing it, I'd shifted so close to him that our chests were nearly touching and my free hand was resting on his shoulder to keep my balance. "Your um, tag was sticking out," I explained lamely, hastily tucking it into the back of his shirt, my fingers brushing lightly against his skin before I pulled away.

Before I could retreat fully, one of his hands shot out and gripped my wrist, his hold gentle as he stared at me. There was a loud boom from the house across the street, making me flinch and Grayson's face hardened into sharp angles once more.

"Promise me you'll never come back here. Whether Paige is here or not."

I bit my lip. "I promise to call you first."

He shook his head, his lips twitching as amusement finally pierced the darkness in his eyes. "Stubborn."

I shrugged. "Yeah."

"You should get going," he said after a long moment, slowly releasing his hold on my wrist.

I nodded, turning to pull open the car door. I paused before climbing in, something keeping me from leaving him just yet.

"Grayson?" I said, facing him once more. His eyes were on me but his attention was elsewhere. Every muscle in his body was still tense and his face was a play of angles and shadows. Did he plan on going back inside?

"What is it, Cupcake?" he asked after I was silent for a long moment.

Just let it go, Nell. He'll be fine.

"Do you need a ride somewhere?" I asked, totally not letting it go.

His lips tilted into a crooked grin and he took a step closer to me. "Worried about me again, Cupcake?" I narrowed my eyes and shook my head. "No? You sure?" I opened my mouth to reply but suddenly, he closed the distance between us, planting one hand on the open door of my car and the other on the roof, his big body surrounding me and making whatever I was going to say lodge in my throat. "You do realize that I can take care of myself, don't you, Nell?"

"Of course," I said, hoping I sounded more indignant than breathless. "I was offering you a ride, Grayson. That's all."

"That's sweet," he said, his voice low, his eyes locked on mine. "Does this mean we're friends now, Cupcake?"

My lips parted but I didn't know what to say to that. Were we friends? Was Grayson West my...friend? It seemed impossible. He'd been nice to me a few times and I didn't doubt that if I ever was in a similar situation as the one I was in tonight, he'd help me out but...

Why would he want to be friends with someone like me?

He rode around on a motorcycle, flipping the bird to anyone who gave him shit. He laughed in people's faces when they disapproved of him.

And I...

I had panic attacks and a cupboard full of pills and a laundry list of supposed neuroses that were casually jotted down on my permanent file like a curse.

Yet, despite everything, I felt comfortable around him, like I could say whatever came to mind without worrying that he'd judge me on it. I'd already stuck my foot in my mouth more times than I'd like to admit around him and he was still there.

Did that make us friends?

I sucked in a breath to reply but suddenly he was gone, his arms no longer caging me in, his expression cold as he looked somewhere over my right shoulder.

"I guess that answers that," he said, crossing his arms over his chest and shooting me a mirthless grin. "I'll see you around, Nell."

I frowned as he turned his back on me, walking towards a line of parked cars, stopping beside his motorcycle and swinging his leg over it. I watched as he started the bike and took off down the street, the usually deafening sound of the vehicle barely even registering compared to the party going on a few feet away.

I got in my car and looked over at the house for a second, breathing a sigh of relief that Grayson hadn't gone back in there. Maybe he looked the part, especially when his eyes went molten and his features turned to granite, but I couldn't shake that feeling that Grayson didn't belong in a place like that.

When I pulled into the driveway fifteen minutes later, Brian's car was parked where mine usually went. I stopped on the road, pulling as close to the curb as I could get before cutting the ignition.

Gritting my teeth, I got out of the vehicle and walked towards the house only, when I reached for the doorknob, it twisted before I could grip it and the door swung open from the inside.

"Nell, baby," Brian said, flashing his teeth as he took a step outside and closed the door behind him. "You just getting home? Did you have fun at the party?" he asked, chuckling at my expense.

"Get out of my way," I muttered, inwardly cursing when my voice came out weak.

"No," he said simply, shifting to block my path as I tried to push around him. "Can't we talk, Nell? It's been ages since we've talked."

We used to talk, Brian and I, when he was still the captain of the football team, before his knee injury. He was nice to me though I suspected it was more to do with the fact that he was dating my sister and Paige and I were a lot closer then. "Not tonight," I said, gritting my teeth when my chest tightened and the beginnings of panic sank into my skin. There was something in his eyes that made me think I didn't want to be alone with him right now.

"Why not?" Brian asked, reaching out and gripping my bicep hard enough to leave a mark. "We used to get along, didn't we, Nell?" he whispered, bringing his free hand to my face, dragging his fingertips along my cheek and down my throat until they came to rest at my collarbone. He tipped his head to the side and I caught a whiff of whiskey on his breath. This close, I could see the white powder clinging to his skin around his nose. He was drunk and high and I seriously needed to make him let go of me. "I guess that was before you lost your mind, wasn't it, Nellie?"

I winced, the tightness in my chest making it hard to breathe. Relax, Nell. You're fine.

"Let me go, Brian," I wheezed.

His grip on my arm tightened and I bit my lip to keep from crying out. "You think you're better than me?" he snarled, his smile vanishing as he pressed his hand to my chest and pushed me against the brick wall hard enough to knock the wind out of me.

I gasped, fighting for oxygen, my fear working against me as my vision went a little hazy for a second. Finally, I managed to suck in some air and when my eyes cleared, Brian was looming over me, his handsome features twisted and ugly, his mouth closing in on mine.

"Don't act like you haven't thought about it, Nell," he sneered lowering his hand until his fingers were brushing my breast.

"Don't," I whimpered, trying to break free of his hold but he was a lot stronger than me.

"Just one kiss. With your hair down like this, you almost look normal. Are you as frigid as you seem, Nellie?"

I jerked my head to the side when he moved his lips towards mine and he lifted his hand from my breast to grip my chin.

"Stop it!" I shouted, my free hand moving quickly, connecting with his cheekbone hard enough to shock him, hard enough to break his hold on me.

Hard enough to fucking hurt.

I didn't think about the pain in my knuckles as I stumbled away from him, my heart beating wildly. I backed up, keeping my hands raised in front of me, fear and panic tumbling through me in waves. Would he hit me back?

He was holding his cheek, his eyes wide in shock as he watched me move towards the street, looking like he was just waking up from a dream.

"Nell, jesus, I'm sorry. I don't know what I was thinking. I didn't me an…" he trailed off, shaking his head hard, lashing out with his fist and connecting with the brick wall with a sickening thud. I thought I heard something crack but he didn't flinch. "Stop," he said after a moment, his voice dead, devoid of emotion as he moved towards the lawn, keeping several feet between us. "I'm leaving," he said, walking out onto the street, leaving his car in the driveway.

I didn't stick around to watch. I bolted inside, closing and locking the door behind me, adrenaline and fear mixing in my blood, making my hands shake furiously.

My ragged breathing echoed around the empty foyer and followed me as I ran up the stairs, lurching into my bedroom and closing the door firmly behind me.

I propped the chair from my desk against the door, wishing I had a lock, bitter that my status as a mental patient didn't allow such luxuries.

My legs crumpled beneath me, my ass hitting the carpet with a muffled thud. My mind was going a thousand miles a minute but I couldn't think of anything aside from the way he'd held my arm, the way he'd pushed me, the feeling of his fingers on my chin, the image of his mouth coming towards mine.

I shook my head, trying to dispel the memories, lifting a hand to wipe at my cheek where I could still feel his lips as they'd missed my mouth.

I winced when my knuckles protested at the movement. Looking down, I saw that they were swollen, bruising already beginning around the bone.

Something about the sight calmed me down and wiped the images from my mind. I focused on my bruised and swollen knuckles and something like satisfaction welled inside of me. A slow smile slipped across my lips. I'd punched him.

I'd actually punched Brian in the face.

My smile widened as I stood up and made my way into the bathroom, flicking on the light and turning the water onto its coldest setting before thrusting my bruised hand under the tap. My eyes shifted upward, landing on my reflection and my smile vanished. My skin was so pale it was almost translucent. My grey eyes looked huge on my face and there were dark circles beneath them. My hair was wild, untamed and tangled and my fingers itched to smooth it into a bun. I frowned at the slight bruising on my chin where Brian's fingers had gripped me, anger welling inside of me.

Had he ever laid a hand on Paige?

The idea had rage curling in my gut, making my hand under the water fist painfully. I'd punch him again if he was in front of me now.

After my hand was numb, I turned off the water and picked up a brush to work it through my hair. When it was smooth, I pulled it into a high bun, making sure all the strands were smooth and in place before brushing my teeth and washing my face.

I smoothed out my pillow before getting into bed and as I reached over to turn off the light, I shifted the book on my nightstand just slightly so that it was perfectly flush with the edge, my water sitting just a couple inches away, right in the middle of its coaster.

With a sigh, I turned out the light, thinking wryly that maybe I couldn't handle having anything crooked or disorganized in my life, but at least I could punch a guy in the face when he was asking for it.

And I hoped I left a mark.

Chapter 8

"What the fuck, Brian, I was waiting for you to come get me. Where the hell are you?" Paige screeched into her cell phone as we pulled up to the school parking lot.

I glanced over at her, a slight chill running down my spine as she mentioned his name. My hands tightened around the steering wheel and I flinched, forgetting that my knuckles were swollen and bruised.

I pulled into a spot and Paige was out of the car before it was even in park. The passenger door slammed and I watched in my rear-view mirror as she stomped away from me.

"Bye," I said into the silence, feeling drained all of a sudden. Would it always be like this between us?

I shook off the thought, gathering my bag from the back seat before heading towards the school. Mentally, I reviewed the homework I'd done over the weekend, making sure I had it all ready and organized for each class. There was no way I was getting another failing grade this year. My applications had already been delivered to the colleges and even though I'd gotten early acceptance to a few, they'd look at my final marks and they reserved the right to change their minds.

The thought made my breath shorten.

What would my parents think if I didn't get into college? Would they be pissed? Would they laugh?

They'd probably just send me to the institution to get rid of me.

I winced at the thought.

The institution wasn't an option. I was never going back there. Never.

Oh shit, is that the time?

I only had ten minutes to get to class and I liked to be a few minutes early.

I picked up the pace, rounding a corner while looking down at my watch.

Which was probably why I smacked into someone coming from the other direction.

"Jesus, watch where you're going."

"I'm sorry," I mumbled, bending to pick up the notebook I'd forced the other girl to drop.

As soon as I straightened, she snatched it out of my hands, the paper slicing into my finger, making me cringe.

I moved to bypass her but she shifted with me, blocking my path. I frowned before actually looking at the girl. She had long red hair and light brown eyes that were heavily caked in black eyeliner. She was tall, almost as tall as me, with sharp, pretty features that were currently pinched in distaste as she looked me up and down.

"You're that girl," she said after a moment, her tone so acidic that she might as well have said, "You're that piece of shit I stepped on the other day."

"Um," I hedged, my eyes shifting towards the clock. Eight minutes. "Probably."

"You're the girl who keeps panting after Grayson."

I winced, looking at her more closely. I'd seen her before, hanging out with Grayson and his friends. She'd given me a few scornful glances in the past. Nothing too original.

"Excuse me," I said, trying to sidestep her again.

She shifted, still blocking me. I bit my lip, my eyes on the clock.

"A little advice? Give up now, honey. He's so far out of your league, it's laughable."

I frowned, shifting my weight from side to side, wondering vaguely how hard I'd have to body check her to get her to move. "What?" I mumbled, forgetting what she'd said.

Eight minutes.

My feet began to inch to the side, seeing a slight opening. If I just squeezed close to the wall…

"Are you even listening to me?" she asked, her hand reaching out to grip my arm.

I winced, her fingers latching onto the exact spot where Brian had grabbed me the night before. Without thinking, I brought my injured hand up to stop her, wrapping my fingers around her wrist and giving a tug.

She loosened her hold but didn't let me go as her eyes shifting to my hand, obviously seeing the bruising there. Slowly, her gaze traveled to my face, narrowing on my chin where I'd obviously done a poor job of covering up the slight bruises there.

"Jesus girl, what happened to you? Your boyfriend beat you up or something?"

I shook my head, tugging harder on her wrist until she let me go fully. "I have to get to class," I mumbled, finally managing to push past her.

I could feel her eyes on my back until I turned a corner, making it to my locker with three minutes to spare.

The bell was just wringing when I stepped into Mr. Ford's class and I sank into my chair just as he started taking attendance. I was in the middle of laying my pens out on my desk when Mr. Ford called my name. My eyes latched on his just as I mumbled, "Present," but my voice came out squeaky and unsure. There was something in his gaze that made my throat close, something that had my spine straightening and my palms sweating.

Disdain.

The look was gone in a flash but I'd seen it. I'd recognize that look anywhere. People looked at me like that all the time. It was the reason why I tried so hard in school, why I couldn't handle getting bad grades. That one look was the reason why anything less than perfect felt like failure to me.

Because I'd been receiving that look from my parents for most of my life.

And I'd been trying for just as long to change it.

As Mr. Ford continued calling out student's names, my hands automatically flew to my hair, searching for any flyaways, the coil in my chest winding just a little bit tighter.

"Hey," Craig whispered, turning in his seat so he could lean closer to me.

"Hi," I mumbled, giving him a quick smile before my fingers shifted towards my pens, making sure they were perfectly straightened.

"So, my dad wants to set up a meeting with you." I frowned, trying to figure out why the hell Craig's dad would want to meet with me. "For the job, remember?"

I blinked, nodding.

"Anyway, when do you think would be a good time?"

I shrugged, thinking about it when suddenly, Craig was right in front of me, his face pushed close to mine, his eyes latched onto my chin. "Is that a bruise?" His fingers gently brushed across my skin and my eyes widened at the contact.

"Um, yeah," I mumbled, pulling back slightly.

"What happened?" he asked, his forehead wrinkled in concern.

"I fell," I whispered, shocked at the genuine concern in his features. "I hit my chin and banged up my hand," I said, showing him the bruises across my knuckles, hoping he didn't think about it too hard. Who fell on their knuckles?

He frowned down at my hand for a second too long before his eyes latched onto mine again. "You sure that's what happened?" he whispered, his face still close to mine.

My eyes widened and my lips parted to reply when Mr. Ford cleared his throat, drawing our gazes.

"Sorry to interrupt but I'm about to begin my class. Or would you prefer we wait?" he asked, his tone laced with condescension.

I straightened in my seat and faced forward. Craig took a second longer but he sank back into his chair, his attention divided between my profile and Mr. Ford.

The rest of the class passed uneventfully. I took meticulous notes, highlighting important parts for studying later.

When the class ended, I packed up my stuff slowly, hoping Craig wouldn't ask me any more questions that I didn't want to answer. My eyes were focused on my pencil case when he said my name. I winced slightly and turned to look at him just as Mr. Ford said, "Miss Watson, can I speak to you for a moment?"

I nodded, tucking the rest of my supplies into my bag before heading to the front of the class, acutely aware of Craig's eyes on me until he slipped out of the room.

"You understand why I gave you a zero on that paper, don't you Nell?"

I nodded, biting the inside of my cheek.

"I couldn't change my policies just because you're usually an exemplary student. I had to treat you just like I treated everyone else. You get it?"

I nodded again, biting my cheek harder. I wanted to argue, to tell him that the paper had been finished, that he didn't have to be such a hard-ass about it.

"Good," he said sternly, picking up a folder and tucking it under his arm. "That being said, I'm willing to give you some extra credit if you're interested."

My eyes latched onto his and I nodded eagerly.

That flash of disdain lit his eyes once more as he handed me a sheet of paper outlining my assignment. "You have until the end of this week, Miss Watson. Don't be late."

"Thank you," I said, giving him a strained smile, finding it hard to shake the feeling that he didn't like me very much. I took the paper and turned my back, heading towards the door.

"Nell?"

Mr. Ford's voice stopped me, my feet freezing in place.

"I won't tolerate any more outbursts from you. Everyone has stress in their lives, everyone has issues that they have to deal with. That doesn't give you an excuse to behave poorly in my class. I won't be giving you special treatment just because of your...situation."

My spine stiffened as bitterness pooled in my gut. Apparently Mr. Ford was aware of my Thursday afternoon therapy sessions.

"I never asked for special treatment, Mr. Ford," I said, my voice coming out tense, unsteady.

"That's good. Then I trust you won't be displaying your dramatics again."

Dramatics? He thought I was just being dramatic? If he knew what it felt like, if he experienced that choking panic that I felt whenever I thought I might be late, when I thought that my paper wasn't going to get a good grade, when I thought my fucking hair wasn't in the right place, would he still feel that way?

I bit my lip to keep from responding.

"You're excused, Miss Watson."

I nodded and with stiff steps, I left the room.

Grayson

"She'll be running soon, I know it. I just gotta find a rad for her and she'll be all good." Dan said animatedly, his grin wide, his hands flying as if he was imagining touching his precious car. "You coming into the shop later or are you working?" Dan asked me.

I grunted, not really paying attention to what he was saying. My mind was focused somewhere else. Or if I was being more honest, on someone else.

Dan started talking again and I gave up on even pretending to listen. Instead, I thought about Nell and the boiling rage that had run through me from the moment I spotted her at that party last night. What the fuck had she been thinking? Nell didn't belong in a place like that. Ever.

I didn't give a shit whether her sister was there or not. If I ever saw her in a place like that again, I'd lose my shit.

I winced slightly, thinking about what I'd almost done to Vin when I'd seen him with his hands on her. I'd come very close to losing my shit on him in a bad way.

Thankfully it hadn't gotten to that point. For once, the way people feared me actually worked in my favour and I hadn't had to smash Vin's face in for laying his hands on Nell.

"Dude, are you even listening to me?"

I blinked over at Dan, realizing he'd been talking this whole time. "No."

He shrugged. "Okay."

Then he kept talking and I continued to tune him out.

My gaze shifted across the parking lot to where Nell's car was parked, my eyes narrowing on the yellow and rusty piece of shit. I needed to stop thinking about her. I'd barely slept last night, my brain turning over and over what had happened once we were alone, away from the party.

The fucked up thing was, I didn't think she even realized she was doing it. One second she was standing there next to me, arguing with me, and the next second she had stepped close to me, so close that we were almost touching and her fingers were sliding along the collar of my shirt, brushing along my skin, just under the fabric of my shirt until they came to rest at the nape of my neck.

I'd almost kissed her then. I'd almost leaned in and pressed my lips to hers.

My lips twisted wryly and I pushed my hand through my hair again, tugging out a few strands. It was good that I hadn't given in, good that I hadn't closed the distance between us. She probably would've passed out. She'd made it abundantly clear that we were nothing to each other. She wouldn't even call us friends for fuck sake.

Girls like Nell Watson didn't give a shit about guys like me. I needed to get that into my head so I could get her out.

I had other shit to worry about with Pierce out of jail.

"You're not even hearing me, are you?"

I blinked, looking over at Dan. "No."

"Jesus, who pissed in your cornflakes this morning?" I shrugged, not bothering to answer. "Aw, poor baby, did you have a bad sleep? Widdle baby want a nappy noodle?"

"Fuck off," I grumbled.

"I would but I'm enjoying the show," Dan said, his eyes focused on something in the distance, his lips tilted into a satisfied grin.

I followed the direction of his gaze, seeing Celine walking in this direction, her hips swaying exaggeratedly, her top cut low enough to see her bra. With long red hair and big, pouty lips, she was hot and she knew it.

And for some reason I couldn't muster any interest in her.

Dan let out a low whistle of appreciation when she got closer and Celine grinned at him before blowing him a kiss. He pressed a hand to his chest, leaning further against the picnic table.

"Hey," Celine said, lowering her voice seductively as she sat between us, turning towards me and brushing her tits against my arm.

I nodded in answer, checking my phone to see how much longer we had for lunch. Twenty minutes.

"What did you do last night?" she asked, running her fingers down my arm.

"Nothing," I mumbled, my eyes on the doors to the school. Maybe I should go in and get Nell to look over my lab report for chem…

"Well, what are you doing tonight? I was thinking we could go for a ride somewhere, have a little fun," she said close to my ear.

"I don't think so," I said distractedly.

"What about tomorrow?"

I made a vague sound in the back of my throat, already forgetting what she'd asked me.

"Jesus," she huffed, dropping the lowered voice. "You and that little girlfriend of yours are the same. Neither of you can pay attention worth shit."

"What?" I snapped, my eyes latching onto hers.

Her eyebrow quirked and her lips twisted sardonically. "Now you pay attention." She shrugged. "I ran into that chick who's always drooling over you this morning. She was so distracted that I don't think she heard a word I said."

"What did you say to her?" I snarled.

Her eyes narrowed. "I just told her the truth. That you're out her league. That she doesn't have a chance with someone like you so she might as well stop following you around like a little puppy."

My fists clenched and I stood up quickly, walking away from the picnic table without a backward glance.

"Hey!" Celine shouted after me but I didn't pause.

I pushed the door to the school open harder than was necessary, making it slam off the door stop, startling a couple of students standing nearby. Some of them looked in my direction before averting their gazes nervously.

Right now, they had every right to be scared of me. I was pissed. At Celine, at Pierce…at Nell.

Had she listened to Celine? Had she promised to stay away from me from now on?

My jaw clenched so hard at the thought, it felt like I chipped a tooth.

I turned a corner, heading towards her locker when I spotted her amongst the crowd of students coming from the other direction.

She was looking down, reading a piece of paper she was holding. Her hair was pulled tight into its usual bun, her forehead was wrinkled in concentration and her white teeth were biting into her bottom lip.

I slowed down, my anger evaporating as I watched her make her way closer to me. I made it to her locker first and I felt my lips tilting up in the corners when she looked up and caught sight of me.

Then she did the last thing I'd expected her to do.

She fucking smiled at me.

And it felt like someone kicked me in the chest.

Mine.

I blinked, ignoring the inane thought as she came closer to me, her lips still stretched into that grin that was threatening to lay me flat.

"Hey," she said, stopping in front of me. "What are you doing?"

"I was looking for you, Cupcake."

She tilted her head to the side, her grin fading slightly but not enough to get rid of the appealing dimple in her cheek. "Why?"

I opened my mouth to reply, my eyes shifting from her dimple to her lips before a shadow caught my attention.

I frowned, my back going ramrod straight as I took a step closer to her, my hands going to either side of her jaw before I'd even realized I was moving.

"Grayson w-wha——"

"What the fuck, Nell?" I rasped, my eyes on the small, finger shaped bruises on her chin.

She lifted her free hand to rest on my forearm, trying to get me to release my hold. "Grayson, it's not——"

"Did someone fucking touch you, Nell?" I snarled, my eyes locked on hers, the grey going molten as she stood there, neither confirming nor denying. Then her attention shifted to her hand, the one that was gripping my forearm and I followed her gaze.

I sucked in a sharp breath at the sight of her bruised and swollen knuckles, pure rage flowing through my veins, making my blood boil. "Who?" I asked, not even recognizing my own voice as I slowly let her go, taking a step back so that I wouldn't be tempted to touch her. I didn't think I could be gentle right now.

"I fell and——"

"I asked you who did this, Cupcake," I repeated, my voice surprisingly steady considering how badly I wanted to punch something.

"What are you going to do if I tell you?" she asked after a moment.

"I'm going to beat the shit out of him, Nell," I replied calmly.

She frowned, shaking her head.

"You will tell me."

She stiffened, her spine straightening in determination. "It's none of your business."

"Really?" I snapped, leaning closer to her. "Because it fucking feels like it's my business."

"Just let it go," she said, turning towards her locker and spinning the lock with jerky movements.

"I'm not letting it go," I said through gritted teeth, my fists resting uselessly at my sides. "You're really not going to tell me?"

She shook her head, taking a couple books from her locker.

"Then I guess I'll just figure it out myself," I snarled, turning my back on her, heading towards the back of the school.

"Grayson!" she called after me but I ignored her, too caught up in my own head. Someone had laid their hands on her. Someone had put fucking marks on her skin.

If she thought I'd just sit back and accept that, she was so fucking wrong.

She'd left right after the party, so the options of who it could be were limited. It could be her little boyfriend, Craig or one of her family members. I didn't particularly relish the thought of beating Nell's dad to a bloody pulp but if he'd touched her...

My vision went red at the thought.

I'd find the annoying football player first. He was always hanging around her. Even if he didn't do it, maybe she'd told him who had.

The thought brought a sour taste to my mouth.

I needed to calm down. On a subconscious level, I recognized that I needed to calm down but it was kind of hard when all I could see were the bruises on her skin and the swelling around her knuckles. The rage flowing through me seemed endless.

I stepped outside, heading towards where the smokers usually hung out. I just needed a second to think and the people back here were usually too stoned to notice when anyone else was around.

Besides, I'd seen Craig back there a couple times, trying to convince his buddy, Brian to get his life back on track.

And if Craig had been the one to touch her, this was the perfect place to kick his ass. No windows, no supervision, no interruptions.

My knuckles cracked as my fists tightened.

Rounding a corner, my gaze shifted over the people gathered around, sharing a joint. Brian was there but no Craig. My eye twitched in irritation as I scanned the stoners around me once more, hoping I'd missed him but I hadn't. I was about to turn back when Brian shifted slightly and I noticed that one of his hands was in a cast. With his un-casted hand, he lifted a smoke to his lips and took a long drag, finishing it off. Flicking the butt, he turned towards me until I could see the other side of his face.

The side with the bruise on his cheekbone.

My eyes narrowed on him and my teeth gritted hard.

Gotcha.

Nell

Oh shit, oh shit, oh shit.

What the hell just happened?

One second, I was standing there, grinning like an idiot at the guy I wasn't supposed to be seen in public with and the next, he was threatening bodily harm to whoever had touched me.

He'll be suspended.

I shook my head, my legs moving fast to try to catch up to him but somehow I'd lost him around the last corner.

What was I so worried about? What were the odds of him figuring out it was Brian anyway?

Slim, right? Very slim.

Still...

I had a sinking feeling in my gut that odds didn't mean shit and Grayson was about to do something he could get into serious trouble for.

Because of me.

I exited through a back door and found him just in time to watch Grayson's fist smash into Brian's face, sending him sprawling across the ground.

My mouth fell open when blood started streaming from Brian's nose but Grayson didn't seem bothered by it. Reaching down, he grabbed Brian by the collar of his shirt, tugging him up until they were face to face. "You know about my reputation, Brian?" Grayson snarled, his face hard, unforgiving.

Brian swallowed and nodded, making a weird whimpering sound.

"Good," Grayson continued, his voice completely calm now. "If you ever lay a hand on Nell again, I won't stop at a broken nose, you understand?" Brian nodded fervently before Grayson released him, letting him fall back onto the ground with a thump.

Brushing his hands off, Grayson straightened, turning his head slightly until his eyes collided with mine.

There was a flash of something in his gaze, regret? But it was only there for a second before it was gone and his black eyes went completely flat. He came towards me but when he got close, he just stepped around me, heading back into the building. I spun on my heel, jogging to catch up to him.

"What the hell, Grayson?" I snapped, glaring over at him.

"Don't act like he didn't deserve it," he replied through gritted teeth. "He's lucky I stopped at a broken nose."

"You didn't even know it was him!" I half shouted, glad the hallway was pretty much deserted.

His steps slowed and his dark eyes flashed over to me. "Are you saying it wasn't?"

My mouth snapped shut and my gaze slid to the side.

"You don't need to confirm it, Cupcake." His voice lowered and his eyes went dark. "He knew what I was talking about."

"I wouldn't exactly call that talking," I hissed.

He came to a stop, turning to face me fully. "Would you prefer I reasoned with him? Would you like it better if I'd asked him politely to never fucking touch you again?"

"I had it under control," I seethed, poking him in the chest.

He snorted.

Something inside of me snapped.

"You know what, Grayson? Fuck you," I snarled, pressing my hands to his chest and shoving. He took a step back, Probably more out of shock than anything else. "You don't get to judge me. You don't get to think that I can't take care of myself because you know what? I did."

"Nell," he said, a muscle in his jaw ticking when I pressed against his chest again and he retreated another step. "You need to stop pushing me now."

"No," I said, pushing him again until his back was resting against a row of lockers. His nostrils flared and his eyes went molten as I stepped closer to him, getting in his space. "I need you to pay attention. You weren't there last night, Grayson." He flinched slightly, his lips tightening. "You couldn't jump in and save me, there was no one else around to protect me and you know what? That's okay. Maybe I don't say much. Maybe I can't handle things being messy or out of order but at least I know now that when it matters, I can punch some asshole in the face."

"He hurt you," Grayson ground out. "He needed to know that's not okay."

I shook my head. "You can't just go around punching people at school!"

He shrugged. "I saw an opportunity. I wasn't going to let that go."

I blew out a frustrated breath. "I don't want you getting suspended because of me, Grayson. Not for something stupid like this."

"Stupid?" he snapped, his features sharpening. "You think it was stupid for me to look out for you?"

"It wasn't necessary. I had it under control."

"Oh, it was necessary. He needed to know that he can't ever touch you again. And I needed to know that the message was received."

Annoyed, I pushed on his chest again, pissed that he was already pressed against the lockers, that I couldn't make him stumble. Instead, I just glared at him and he glared right back, looking equally pissed at me.

Finally, he sighed, some of the tension fading from his features. "Look, I'm not saying you didn't do good, punching him in the face, Cupcake. I'm impressed as hell that you gave him that shiner but whether you had it under control or not, I needed to make sure that it wouldn't happen again." Slowly, he reached up, brushing his fingers lightly over the bruises on my chin and his expression warmed a few degrees. "I don't like seeing you hurt, Nell."

And just like that, the fight seeped out of me.

"Oh," I said, my voice coming out embarrassingly breathy. His touch was doing something to me. The feeling of his skin on mine was making my heart race and my knees shake. I needed to move away from him but the way he was looking at me right now was keeping my feet locked in place.

Someone slammed their locker a few feet away, making me jump slightly, bringing me back to earth. I took a step back from Grayson in an attempt to clear my head but I had to fight not to lean closer to him again when he stopped touching me.

Before he lowered his hand, I reached out and grabbed it, inspecting his knuckles critically. "How come it's not bruised?"

"I hit him in the nose," he said, his voice hoarse. "It's mostly cartilage. Makes for a softer impact."

I nodded, brushing my finger across his knuckles once before grinning up at him. "Next time I'll aim for the nose."

His forehead wrinkled. "There won't be a next time, Cupcake."

I shrugged. "Just in case."

He shook his head, the wrinkles on his brow multiplying until a lock of hair slipped down to cover them. Without thinking, I shifted closer to him, going up on my tiptoes the brush his hair back into place. As soon as my fingers touched his forehead, we both froze.

My lips parted and my eyes widened but I couldn't seem to tear my gaze from his.

Back off, Nell. Now.

I couldn't move. There was something stopping me from shifting away, something keeping me close to him, wanting to be closer, and it sizzled between us.

His chest was rising and falling rapidly, his eyes were molten pools of black as he stared down at me. "Nell?" he rasped.

With a slight gasp, I pulled my hand away from his face, stumbling back a step at the same time.

"Sorry," I mumbled, cheeks blazing. I avoided his eyes as I smoothed my hand down my t-shirt before shoving my hand into my jean's pocket just in case I did something stupid. Like touch him again.

"Nell," he repeated, his voice gruff as he took a step towards me but he stopped when I immediately backed away.

My lips curled into a stiff smile. "I need to get to class," I said, my tone flat, controlled.

My eyes caught on his hand, his fingers curling into a fist just before I turned my back on him and began power walking away.

I'd retrieved my books and was almost at my class by the time I'd managed to convince myself that it wasn't such a big deal. Grayson probably hadn't thought anything of it and I was blowing everything out of proportion. So I'd stepped super close to him and brushed his hair to the side. Who cared?

Not me.

Nope.

I walked into class and took my seat, organizing my pens and pencils, pretending that nothing was different, that nothing had changed, that if I hadn't stepped away from him when I did, I wouldn't have done something colossally stupid.

Like found out what it felt like to kiss Grayson West.

Because if I was being honest with myself, I'd admit that from the moment I stepped close to him until the moment I moved away, that was the only thing I could think about.

And even though it was ridiculous and made no sense, I couldn't seem to stop thinking about it.

Chapter 9

Nell

The sound of shattering glass made me wince but I forced myself to ignore it as I went over my Spanish homework.

Someone yelled "Opa!" just before more glass broke and I gripped the arms of the chair I was sitting on to keep from going down there.

My parents were out of town. Naturally to Paige, that translated to party.

Even though they were only gone for one night, considering how many people had piled in the front door in the past few hours, the clean up was going to be atrocious.

Shaking my head, I forced myself to concentrate on the notebook in front of me. I was finally able to drown out the sound of whatever top forty hit that was playing when there was a knock on my door.

I squeezed my eyes shut in irritation and pushed myself up from my desk, fully expecting to find a horny couple looking for a bed on the other side of my door.

What I wasn't expecting to find was my sister, alone aside from a bottle of tequila and two red solo cups.

"You coming to party, Nellie?" she asked, pushing past me without waiting for my answer.

I winced as she flopped onto my bed.

Her brow quirked as she bent her elbow and propped her head on her hand. "Oh, I'm sorry, did I wrinkle the sheets?" she asked, her words a little slurred.

I didn't reply because that was exactly why I'd winced and she really didn't need more ammunition against me.

She laughed, swinging her legs over the side of the bed and planting the bottle on my nightstand before separating the two cups and placing them in front of the bottle. "Want a drink?" she asked, already adding tequila to both glasses.

"I think you've had enough," I said, noting that she'd doled out the liquor with a heavy hand.

She snorted, leaning back against the headboard. "You're such a party pooper, Nell." She took a swig from her cup, smacking her lips together when she was done. "C'mon," she said, reaching for the other cup and holding it out to me.

I took it, holding it with both hands to make sure it didn't spill. When she looked at me expectantly, I sent a frown towards the golden liquid before bringing it to my lips and taking a tiny sip.

"That's disgusting," I gasped when the liquor hit my tongue and burned its way down my throat.

"Yup," she said in reply, taking another swig, her eyes shifting back to my nightstand, coming to rest on the framed picture I had there.

Her mouth pinched tighter and her eyes narrowed as she reached towards it and picked the frame up, examining the picture like she'd never seen it before.

It was the two of us a few years ago. I was fourteen and she was thirteen when it was taken. We'd spent the day at an amusement park, just the two of us and had asked someone to take a photo of us. Both of our noses were a little burnt from the sun but our smiles were wide and genuine. Our arms were linked and we were leaning towards each other, almost against each other like the one couldn't stand without the other.

It was my favourite picture of the two of us.

"When did everything get so fucked up?" Paige said in a quiet voice laced with pain.

My eyes widened and I took a step towards her. "Paige——"

She shook her head, slamming the picture onto the nightstand, facedown. "Drink with me, Nell," she said, any emotion in her voice gone now.

"We should talk," I rasped, my heart aching with the need to talk to her, to get back to where we were in that picture.

"No, we should drink. Just have a drink with me," she said, her blue eyes bright and a little bit bloodshot as they connected with mine.

It was the hint of desperation in her voice that had me tilting the cup towards my lip again, taking a deep swallow.

She shot me a grin as a reward, lifting her cup in my direction before finishing off her own.

Leaning over, she grabbed the bottle to refill before getting off the bed and walking around the room.

Her fingers trailed across my things, leaving her touch on everything, her sharp eyes missing nothing as she passed by my dresser, noting the lack of dust, eyeing the symmetrical placement of my bobby pins and necklaces. When she reached my desk, she looked down at my notes with a speculative eye, her fingers reaching towards my pens, counting the three blue, two black and one red before shifting to the highlighters.

I looked away as she inspected my things, finding it hard to just sit there while she judged me.

"It was never this bad before," she said, moving to my closet and opening the doors, seeing the way I'd organized my clothes first by colour, then by style. "You've gotten worse."

I shrugged, standing and moving towards her, reaching around her to close my closet, embarrassment and tequila making my cheeks red.

"Mom did that to you," she said, her words making me freeze, my eyes latching onto her.

She didn't seem to notice my intense regard as she moved back to my bed and sat down. "She was always so hard on you, demanding perfection. Remember when you were taking piano?" My spine stiffened and I moved towards the chair as the memory of my mother and piano lessons flashed through my consciousness.

"She hated when you got it wrong but I think she hated it even more when you got it right," Paige continued softly, her eyes on the carpet in front of her.

I gritted my teeth against the wave of remembered panic that threatened to overtake me. Shaking my head, I tipped the cup towards my mouth, eager to get rid of that memory.

"I wanted to protect you, did you know that?" Paige asked, a wry smile curling her lips as she looked over at me. She rolled her eyes as she took another swig, wiping the excess moisture from her lips with the back of her hand as she lowered the cup. Her features turned hard for a second as she stared at me before rolling her eyes. "There I was thinking we were a team while you turned around and betrayed me."

I cringed. "It wasn't like that——"

"Brian's been acting weird lately," she interjected, her eyes on the wall now, no longer focused on me, on us. "He hasn't been returning my calls and he didn't even show up tonight."

"Maybe that's a good thing," I said hesitantly. "Maybe it wouldn't hurt if things between you and Brian cooled off."

Paige's gaze landed on me and sharpened. "You think we should break up, is that it?"

I shrugged, knowing from the way her eyes were narrowed and her shoulders were squared that there was no right answer at this point.

"You never did understand why I love him," she snarled, lurching to her feet.

"Paige, that's not——"

"Oh, just fuck off, will you? You're just jealous because we're great together and you have no one."

I opened my mouth to deny it but she was already out of my room, the door slamming hard in her wake.

Frustrated, I stood, tipping the last of the contents in my cup down my throat, enjoying the burn as I paced around my room, absentmindedly reaching out to push things that Paige had moved back into their positions.

Moving back to the bed, I sat down, reaching towards the picture of the two of us. Longing rushed through me as I looked at the girls in the picture, wishing I could go back to being that girl.

When was the last time I'd felt that carefree? When was the last time I'd been able to let go like that? To smile like that?

With a sigh, I put the picture back in its place, pushing on the frame slightly to make sure it was at a forty five degree angle from the edge of the table.

You've gotten worse.

She was right. Even if I couldn't see it, even if she hadn't laid it out for me, I could feel it. The tension that lived in my bones never seemed to ease anymore. The desperate need for everything to be just so was constant.

I stood up, pacing the foot of my bed as I thought about my piano lessons, about the way my hands would shake whenever my mother was watching, the way she'd yell whenever I messed up. The day she'd finally given in and declared me hopeless was one of the happier memories of my life.

I hadn't touched a piano since.

But that didn't mean I wasn't still trying, and failing, to earn my parent's approval. What was it going to take?

Nothing. There is nothing I can do to change it.

I cringed at the thought, my eyes catching on my reflection in the mirror above my dresser and holding. The tension around my eyes was obvious, the stiff set of my shoulders and steel in my spine made me look like I was ready to go into battle, not settling down for a night of Spanish verb conjugations.

Closing my eyes, I turned away from my reflection, pulling at the elastic holding my hair in place. I needed a break. I needed a moment or two to just be Nell, to not worry about what other people might think, what my parents might read into my behaviour, what my shrink might see when she looks at me.

I used to get that when I was around Paige. I used to be able to let go when it was just the two of us but I screwed that up. I hurt her and I was starting to think forgiveness wasn't forthcoming.

With a sigh, I walked towards the bed, brushing the wrinkles out of the comforter and readjusting the pillows until they were right.

I was contemplating my work when my phone buzzed in my pocket and I absentmindedly pulled it out.

Grayson: Remember what I said, Cupcake. If you pick up your sister, I'm going with you.

I narrowed my eyes at the message, ignoring the way my lips were sort of twitching, like I wanted to smile.

Me: Don't call me Cupcake.

I pressed send, letting my smile spread for a moment, some of the tension easing out of my shoulders.

Grayson: I swear to god, Nell, if you went to a party without calling me...

I swallowed hard, thinking about the last party I'd stepped into because of my sister, thinking about the guy who I wasn't so sure would've let me go if it hadn't been for Grayson.

Me: Relax, I'm doing Spanish homework. The party's at my house tonight so no rescue mission necessary.

I was about to put my phone down when something made me freeze, some stupid, insane urge overcame me to the point where I was typing a new message, barely even considering what I was doing before I pressed send.

Me: You can come over if you want.

"Idiot," I mumbled, smacking myself in the forehead before throwing the phone onto my bed. "What the hell is wrong with me?" I'd just invited Grayson to my house. As in the den of the beast, as in, if my parents ever found out, I'd have a one way ticket to an institution of their choosing before you could say the word, tequila.

Which was the only explanation for why I'd invited Grayson West to my house. Tequila. There was no way I'd have done it if I were sober. Not a chance.

...I'm pretty sure.

I cringed slightly at the thought before brushing it off. What did it matter anyway? It's not like he would say yes. It was Friday night. He was probably at a party with his own fr——

My phone beeped.

I blinked at the offending device, cursing myself even as I reached for it.

Grayson: Be there in ten minutes.

My fingers hovered over the screen long after it went black, trying to convince myself that I needed to text him back, to call him off, to tell him it was a mistake.

But I couldn't.

Instead, I just sat there, staring at the device until about ten minutes later, I heard the telltale sound of a motorcycle roaring down the street.

Flinging my phone onto the bed, I moved to my window and pushed it open, leaning my head out just as he pulled into the driveway.

He cut the engine and pulled his helmet off, his eyes shifting unerringly up until they landed on me.

"Hey Cupcake," he said, his lips tipping up in one corner.

I attempted to scowl but it was hard to do with the smile trying to force its way onto my mouth. "Don't call me that," I said, my reprimand lacking heat.

He shrugged, swinging his leg off the bike and gesturing to the door. "Should I let myself in?"

"Yeah," I said without hesitation, my plan to tell him to leave evaporating in an instant. "I'll meet you downstairs."

Turning my back on the window, I walked out of my room and down the stairs, spotting Grayson as he came into the foyer, his eyes scanning the people milling about for a second before landing on me.

I stopped fighting the grin, letting it bloom across my lips as I made it to the bottom of the stairs, pushing past a few people to reach him.

I should've probably said something but my brain was too busy trying to figure out how to operate. My gaze ran over his tousled hair, his five o'clock shadow and his black t-shirt that clung to his chest in a way that had my throat going dry.

Mentally shaking my head, I tried to focus and was about to say something when someone bumped into me from behind, forcing me to take a step closer to Grayson. His hands came up, resting lightly on my biceps while his lips tipped into a crooked grin. "Have you been drinking, Nell?" he asked, raising one hand to trail his fingers across my cheek. "You're flushed."

I shrugged, not bothering to answer him. Or maybe I wasn't able to with the way my throat had closed when his fingers had touched my skin.

I cleared my throat and took a step back from him, jerking my head in the direction of the kitchen. "Want a drink?" I asked.

His shoulders lifted and he followed me as I wound my way through the people crowded into the hallway.

My breath started coming a little faster as I brushed up against sweaty bodies.

Chill, Nell. You're fine.

I took a deep breath, the scent of spilled beer and something minty climbing up my nose, making me cringe but for some reason it made the panic recede enough for me to forge ahead, finally making my way into the crowded kitchen.

"Where are the glasses?" Grayson asked, leaning closer to me so he could be heard above the hum of drunken conversation.

I pointed at the counter where the plastic cups were and he nodded, people automatically moving out of his way as he moved in that direction.

"Oh my god," Paige said, suddenly directly in front of me, her eyes dancing with mirth, her lips twisted in a grin. "Did you seriously invite Grayson West to my party?"

I shrugged. "Yes," I said, daring her to argue with me.

She shook her head, giving a light chuckle before leaning closer. "If Mom finds out, you're out of here, you know that right?"

"Then don't tell her," I said, feigning a calm I wasn't exactly feeling.

She looked at me steadily for a minute before shrugging her shoulders. "Fine. Just tell him to keep his hands to himself. If anything gets stolen, I'll know who to blame it on."

"He's not like that," I snapped through gritted teeth, anger pooling in my belly.

She rolled her eyes, turning slightly so she could look him up and down as he walked towards us. "Don't delude yourself, Nell. He might look good in a pair of jeans but he doesn't belong within ten feet of this zip code. He's got 'future criminal' written all over him. He's not one of us."

She turned up her nose, obviously judging him beneath her.

"I'm not one of you," I said when he was just a couple feet away, making Paige swing her gaze over to me once more. "In this house, if anyone doesn't belong, it's me."

Something flashed in her eyes, sorrow maybe? But it was gone before I could get a good grip on it and without another word, she turned her back on me, walked out of the kitchen and disappeared into the crowd.

Grayson's eyes had followed her retreat before they slowly swung back to me. A line appeared on his brow as he looked down at me, two red solo cups in either hand. He jerked his head towards the balcony and leaned a little closer. "Want to get some air, Cupcake?" he asked after a second.

I breathed out a sigh and nodded, some of the tension leaving my shoulders as soon as we were headed away from the crowd.

I stepped out onto the patio and immediately felt like I could breathe again.

That is, until a sound drew my attention to the group of five people standing off to the side, their eyes on me, identical condescending grins on their lips as they whispered to one another. I heard the word loser a few times and when they threw the word 'crazy' into the mix, I scowled.

Then everything changed.

The vibe on the deck went from patronizing to terrified in a second and their smirks disappeared as their eyes shifted to something behind me.

Or rather, someone.

I jumped slightly when Grayson planted his hand on my shoulder, his arm circling around my back protectively as he stared down the people standing across from us.

"I think you guys will like it better inside, don't you agree?" Grayson asked with a clear undertone of menace.

It was almost comical the way they rushed to put out their cigarettes, their eyes cast downwards as they shuffled past us and snuck into the house.

When the door was closed and we were alone on the patio, I turned to face Grayson, his hand sliding along my shoulder and across my spine before falling to his side. "People are kind of scared of you, huh?"

His dark eyes locked on mine and he was silent for a long beat before saying, "Not everyone."

I shrugged, reaching out to take one of the two cups he'd manage to carry in his free hand. "What is this?" I asked, bringing it to my nose to smell it.

"Water."

I frowned, leaning forward to look into his, seeing that it was also filled with a clear liquid.

"Both of them," he said, bringing the cup to his lips and taking a sip.

"You could've had a beer or something."

He shrugged, walking towards the railing, leaning a hip against it before turning his gaze back to me. "I'm good."

I nodded just as a loud, tinkling laugh reached my ears and I couldn't help but look behind me into the house. Paige was sitting on the kitchen counter with people surrounding her. I watched as she took a shot someone handed to her then held the empty glass up triumphantly, her grin wide as the crowd cheered.

If that were me, I'd be on the floor having a panic attack.

Just then her eyes shifted and connected with mine through the glass, her lips twisting into a sardonic smile as her chin lifted slightly.

Gritting my teeth I turned away from the window, anger trickling down my spine.

She's already wasted, I thought, hating that she had to put on a show for these people, hating that they loved her for it. They didn't even know her.

Or maybe it was me who didn't know her...

"What's the deal with the two of you?"

I blinked, realizing that Grayson had been watching the whole exchange silently. I shrugged. "Sibling rivalry?"

His brow quirked and he gave me a disbelieving look while I plucked at the hem of my shirt, searching for loose threads. "Is it really that simple, Nell?"

I shrugged, having no intention of telling him anything. I mean, c'mon, I'd embarrassed myself in front of Grayson West enough times already. I really didn't need to add my family drama to——

"She hates me," I blurted before staring blankly at him, disbelief making my eyes wide.

What the fuck, Nell? The plan was to not say anything.

"Why?" Grayson asked, his attention focused entirely on me.

With a sigh, I walked towards him, leaning forward to rest my elbows on the rail next to him, letting my hands dangle over the edge of the porch. "I screwed up. She told me a secret, asked for my help and I…" I winced at the memory. "I fed her to the wolves." With a short laugh, I straightened, shifting to face him. "I don't know why I'm telling you this," I blurted.

He gave me a funny look, his expression unreadable as he tilted his head to the side. "Me neither," he said softly.

A smile slipped onto my lips before I gave my head a slight shake. "What about you? You and Pierce didn't exactly seem like buddies. What's the story?"

His features turned to granite and his spine went ramrod straight. Water sloshed over the edge of his cup as he put it down a little too hard, the bottom crumpling slightly against the railing. His gaze shot to the cup and stayed there as he ran a hand through his hair, making the already messy strands even more so.

"I don't really want to get into that, Nell," he said stiffly, still not looking at me.

"Okay."

His gaze shot to me and he gave me a puzzled look, like he was expecting me to push.

Suddenly, he squared his body to me, his dark eyes completely black. The lines of his face were accented, the shadows from the light at the porch making his cheekbones stand out in relief. He looked like he was about to walk in front of a firing squad.

"Might as well know," he mumbled before swallowing hard and continuing in a flat voice, "My dad was a construction worker. We weren't rich, but there was always food on the table and a roof over our heads. A few years back, he got hurt. Fell off a ladder and broke his back." His forehead wrinkled in remembered worry and I had the insane urge to reach out to him, to grab his hand in mine and offer him comfort.

I put my cup on the railing and shoved my hands into my pockets instead.

"After that, the money stopped coming in and we were going to lose the house. Pierce started selling drugs to help keep us afloat. It worked. But then my dad got better and he went back to work and Pierce didn't stop. He kept getting in deeper and deeper and I didn't stop him."

"Grayson," I said, taking a half step closer to him, not sure what else to say.

Which was right about the time I realized that my hands hadn't stayed in my pockets, that I'd actually reached out and placed my hand on his where it lay on the railing, his fingers clutching the wood until his knuckles had whitened.

He stared down at my hand on his and his lips tightened into a thin line before he shifted away, turning his back on me to pace towards the other side of the deck. "Don't get the wrong idea, Nell. I'm not exactly an innocent in this story." He gave a light chuckle, turning back to me with a blank look on his face and a humourless grin on his lips. "I may not have been the one dealing drugs but when someone had issues paying the money, I was the one they answered to. That's why people are afraid of me, Cupcake. That's why the hallway clears when I walk by."

His gaze shifted to his hands, staring down at the white scars across his knuckles as shadows crossed his eyes. "I used to beat the shit out of people for drug money," he said, his voice flat and when he looked up at me, his features were cut in granite, the smile on his lips stiff and unnatural. "Most people already know. I don't know why you never heard the rumours but I get it if you walk back inside and never speak to me again. I'm not the kind of guy girls like you hang out with."

I frowned, giving my head a slight shake. "I've pissed you off a few times, haven't I?"

He gave me a puzzled look and frowned. "What does that have to do with anything?"

"I've made you mad and you've never laid a finger on me. That——"

"That's not what I'm saying," he said, suddenly right in front of me, his face close to mine. "I would never hurt you, Nell. Ever."

"Then why do you think I'm going to walk away?" I asked, my voice a bit breathy from his proximity.

"Because you should," he replied, his gaze dipping to take in my features, his eyes going a shade darker. "Because if you don't do it now, I'm not giving you another chance."

My lips parted and for one crazy, insane second, I thought he was moving closer to me.

Then the patio door slid open, the sound making me jump back slightly. Craig walked out of the house, his eyes immediately latching onto Grayson and narrowing. "You've been out here a while, Nell. Why don't you come back inside and have a drink with me."

Grayson snorted and crossed his arms over his chest as he took a step to the side, turning so he was facing Craig.

"I don't want to go in there, Craig," I said, glancing over his shoulder at the party going on behind him.

"C'mon, Nell. It's getting cold and your...friend's probably ready to head out." Craig's bloodshot eyes shifted, landing on Grayson. Craig shot him a mocking smile and stepped slightly closer to me, reaching out to wrap his hand around my forearm, giving a light tug. "This isn't exactly your kind of party anyway, right?"

"Craig, stop it," I snapped, wincing when he turned to me, the scent of beer practically escaping his pores. "You're drunk."

He shrugged. "So what? Brian's at home, Paige is in her own house and under control. Don't you think we deserve to have a little fun?" He reached out with his other hand so that he could turn me towards him. "Have a drink with me, Nell," he said softly, his eyes running over my features, a crooked smile on his lips. "I've wanted to talk to you about something."

My forehead wrinkled as I looked up at him, trying to read the intensity in his eyes but I couldn't figure him out. "About what?"

Craig took a deep breath and parted his lips but just then, the patio door slid open and people began to pour out, shoving us to the side until my hip hit the railing and I would've stumbled if someone hadn't wrapped their arm around my waist, keeping me steady.

"You good, Cupcake?" Grayson asked, his mouth close to my ear as people ran towards the steps, shouting at each other and stumbling towards the side of the house.

"I'm good," I mumbled, trying to ignore the shivers going up and down my spine. "What's going on?" I asked, frowning as the crowd thinned leaving only a few stragglers to casually walk out of the house.

"We're busted," a very drunk girl giggled, stumbling towards me and latching onto my arm for support. "The parents came home early. Paige is going to be in so much trouble," she tittered, lurching away from me to walk down the steps.

I blinked a few times, for a long, blissful minute, her words not penetrating.

But then they did.

And I nearly keeled over in panic.

"My parents are home," I wheezed, my vision going grey at the edges as I forgot how to breathe. "Oh my god, it's a mess. I need time. I have to clean this up. I can't——"

"Nell," Grayson said, gripping my shoulders and turning me towards him, his dark eyes locked on mine, his face so close to mine that it was the only thing I could see. "This isn't your party. Paige is the one who's in trouble here. Paige is the one who has to clean this up. If your parents know you at all, they'll know you didn't invite these people here."

I bit my lip and shook my head, my throat closing over any words I may have been trying to form. My mind was racing, images crowding my head of the living room covered in tipped beer cans and garbage that I needed to clean up right now.

Maybe they hadn't seen? Maybe I still had time before——

"Come on, Nell," Craig said, lightly gripping my arm and giving a tug. "I'll go explain to them that this wasn't your party. They'll understand."

"No," I wheezed pathetically, pulling my arm away from him.

I seriously needed my lungs to start working.

"I have to go…in there…I have to…fix this. They're going to——"

I was cut off when a pair of arms suddenly wrapped around my waist and lifted, leaving my feet to dangle off the ground as we moved down the steps to the side of the house.

I blinked when Grayson set me down with my back to the house, my eyes wide as I looked up at his face so close to mine. "Grayson, wha——"

"This. Is not. Your problem, Cupcake. Are you hearing me?"

I flinched, turning my gaze to the side. "You don't understand."

He was silent for a second, his breathing picking up for some reason. When he lifted his hand and touched my chin, guiding it until I was looking at him again, I didn't resist. "I understand that if you go in there and they're yelling at your sister, you'll step in and take the blame. I understand that if I walk away and leave you here, you're going to end up cleaning that entire house by yourself." My heart stuttered when his lips tilted into a crooked grin and his fingers shifted from my chin to my cheek, brushing lightly over the skin there. "So I'm thinking you should come with me."

"What?" I croaked, telling my lips not to smile back at him, that there was nothing about this situation that warranted a goddamn smile.

But when his grin got a little wider, I couldn't help it and I felt my traitorous lips tilting upward.

"We're going to get on my bike and drive around for as long as we feel like it and then we're going to get pancakes. What do you say, Nell Watson? You with me?"

No. I was so not with him. I had to go inside. I had to face the music, talk to my parents, clean the stupid house. There was no way in hell that I was——

"French toast," I heard myself say, my stupid lips already tipping into an even bigger grin. "I want French toast."

His smile widened and he gave a low laugh that had my stomach dipping in that way it does when you go down a drop on a roller coaster and I stopped fighting it.

I wasn't going into that house. I was going to climb on the back of Grayson West's motorcycle and go wherever he'd take me.

And even though I'd expected to be panicked at the thought of leaving Paige in there alone, I wasn't.

In fact, I felt...light. Like there was no coil in my chest, no pressure on my shoulders, no weight sitting on my lungs keeping me from breathing properly.

"C'mon Cupcake," Grayson said, his smile wide as he took a step back and held his hand out for me.

"She's not going with you," Craig said, suddenly appearing next to me, glaring at Grayson.

I blinked, having forgotten that he was nearby.

"That's really not up to you," Grayson said, his smile disappearing as his gaze shifted away from me.

"She barely even knows you. We've been friends for a long time now, I'll take care of her," Craig said, wrapping his fingers around my wrist and giving a light tug.

"Craig, wait," I mumbled, about to pull my wrist out of his hold when someone came around the side of the house.

"There you are," the girl said, her long blonde hair falling in loose waves around her shoulders. I recognized her as one of Paige's friends but I couldn't think of her name. "C'mon Craig, let's get out of here before Paige's parents call the cops on us. We waited for you."

"Nell's coming with us," Craig said, tugging my wrist until I was forced to take a step around Grayson, the moonlight illuminating my features.

I watched as the blonde girl's eyes lit with recognition. "You're joking, right?" she said, laughing.

"No," Craig replied, irritation in his voice.

"I'm going with Grayson," I said before the girl could say anything else.

"Perfect. See Craig, she's got a ride."

"What? You can't be serious, Nell," Craig said, frowning down at me.

"I'll be fine," I replied, forcing a smile onto my lips as I pulled his hand off my wrist. "Go."

"C'mon," the blonde said, reaching for Craig's hand and tugging him along with her. As they neared the front of the house, I heard her say, "What's with you and Paige's crazy sister, anyway?"

I cringed and examined the grass at my feet, hoping Grayson hadn't heard her.

"Cupcake?"

"Yeah?" I responded, still staring at the ground.

"Let's get out of here, okay?"

A smile curved my lips upward and my eyes lifted to his. "Yeah."

"Here," he said, shrugging his jacket off his shoulders before draping it over mine.

"I'm not cold."

"Just in case your parents spot you. This way, they won't recognize you," he said, leaving his arm around my shoulders as he steered me towards the front of the house. "Lean into me, Cupcake. If anyone's looking, we'll look like any other couple. No one will think it's you."

I did as he asked, my side coming into full contact with his as my arm slipped around his waist.

Whoa, was it healthy for my heart to be beating this fast?

I took a deep breath, trying to tell myself that it was no big deal, that I was completely unaffected by the feel of Grayson's body pressed against mine.

"Here," Grayson said when we stopped in front of his bike, shifting so that his back was to the house, his body blocking anyone's view of me if they happened to be looking. He gripped the spare helmet and plopped it on my head, his fingers brushing my chin as he did up the strap.

He made quick work of his own helmet and in seconds, we were both on his bike, my arms wrapped around his waist as the engine roared to life beneath us. I felt a smile stretch across my lips as we lurched forward, my house fading into the darkness behind us. It shouldn't feel like this. It shouldn't feel this...right to be getting away from that place, from my family.

But it did. I couldn't deny the lightness settling into my bones or the way my breathing came more easily now that we were further from my house.

This was probably a mistake. If I couldn't come up with a good reason for my absence from the house tonight, I had no doubt they'd send me away again.

But I couldn't seem to muster the energy to care at the moment. I was wrapped up in the feeling of being on the back of Grayson's bike with the world whipping past, my arms looped around him tightly. Other than the promise of French toast, there was no plan, no colour coded itinerary, no organized schedule of events to follow and at the moment, I couldn't see a single thing wrong with that.

Grayson

"Are you sure about this?" Nell asked as I stashed the helmets back in their compartment, her forehead wrinkled as she examined the hole-in-the-wall diner in front of her.

"Positive," I responded, my lips twitching as I turned towards her, placing my hand at the small of her back and giving a gentle shove to get her moving. "There's nowhere else I'd go for breakfast at four in the morning."

"Is it because this is the only place open at four in the morning?" she mumbled, raising a brow at the flickering sign that had once said Earl's but now only the s was still lit.

"Yup," I replied, grinning down at her as we stood in front of the door. "You backing out, Cupcake?"

"Not a chance. You promised me French toast. I expect you to deliver," she said, stepping away from me and pulling the door open before stepping inside.

My grin widened as I followed her, noting the peeling paint and the faded booths. My gaze slid back to Nell as she sat down, her hand reaching up to smooth out her hair only to find it a tangled mess thanks to the helmet she'd been wearing. After a brief hesitation, she lowered her hand again, giving up.

A sense of satisfaction welled in my gut. There was something great about seeing Nell with her guard down, with her hair messy and her clothes a little wrinkled. It felt like, even though I'd screwed up more times than I could count with this girl, for whatever reason, she seemed to be...comfortable around me.

"Okay, milkshakes first," she said, her lips curling into a grin as I sank into the booth across from her.

"Okay," I replied, helpless against the answering smile that curled my lips. What was it about this girl that got to me?

I was still on the fence, trying to figure out if it had been a good idea or not to go to the Watson mansion. She really did live in the lap of luxury but for all the gilded wallpaper and fancy artwork on the walls, Nell didn't seem changed by it.

She doesn't belong there.

I almost snorted out loud at the thought. Of course she belonged there. I was the one who didn't belong within a hundred yards of a place like that. Hell, I didn't belong within a hundred yards of a girl like Nell.

The thought didn't sit well with me.

"What can I get you?" the waitress asked without preamble, her expression one of abject boredom.

"I'll have a strawberry milkshake and French toast, please."

"I'll get the same," I grunted, my eyes shifting back to Nell, tracking her dimple as she smiled politely at the waitress and handed her our menus.

Nell watched her retreating form for a while, her smile slowly fading until her lips were turned down slightly in the corners, her forehead wrinkled into a frown. Her hands swept over the table, grabbing a roll-up and neatly undoing it, smoothing the napkin out until it was flat, positioning her knife and fork flush with the edge of the table.

Suddenly, she stilled, her shoulders going stiff as her gaze lifted to mine. "I don't get you, Grayson West," she said softly.

"Not much to get, Cupcake," I responded, my voice hoarse in my own ears.

"Why are we here?" she whispered, as if afraid of my answer.

I lifted a brow. "French toast and strawberry shakes?"

She gave one, slow shake of her head. "Not what I meant."

"You're gonna have to catch me up," I replied.

Her gaze raked over my features. "I never expected you to tell me about your past. I wouldn't have pried."

"I know," I rasped through gritted teeth, regretting telling her the truth. Did she see me differently now? Had come with me because it hadn't fully sunk in yet? Was she going to tell me that this was it, that she couldn't stand being near someone like me?

"You deserve the same from me," she croaked, sitting up straighter in her seat, her smile a mere memory now. Her silver eyes had gone flat, her features completely expressionless. "I'm sure you've noticed, but just in case you missed it, people call me crazy."

"They're idiots," I growled, the intensity in my voice catching me off guard just as much as it did her. Her eyes widened and latched onto mine.

Slowly, she shook her head. "They're not entirely wrong." Her shoulders squared and I couldn't help but admire the determination in her gaze. "I'm obsessive compulsive. There are certain things I do that make no sense. I get that they make no sense but I do them anyway because I can't not."

"Okay," I responded, not surprised by her statement. I'd already figured that she had something like OCD. The way she constantly checked her hair, the way she organized her pens…it was obvious.

Her lips parted slightly in shock. "Okay?"

I shrugged but didn't get a chance to say more because the waitress planted our milkshakes and French toast down at that moment.

"Thank you," I said, grabbing my knife and fork and getting ready to dig in. "Eat, Cupcake," I ordered when she still hadn't moved.

Slowly, as if in a daze, she lifted her fork and let the tines land on her toast, puncturing the bread slightly. "I just told you that I'm sick and your response is, 'okay',?"

I shrugged, taking a big bite of the French toast. "What did you think I would say? 'Well, that does it, I can't ever see you again, ever'?" I shook my head and frowned, noticing how pale her face had gone. "Wait, is that what you thought I'd say, Nell?"

Her eyes shifted to the breakfast in front of her. "Mine's a pretty mild case. Stress makes it worse." She took a bite and chewed slowly, her expression distant, thoughtful before she gave her head a light shake. "It's more than that, though. I've got other...issues. I've seen a therapist...a lot." Her teeth pressed into her lower lip as she faced me once again, her eyes locking on mine. "You gave me an out so I'm giving you the same. If you want to turn around and walk out the door right now, I———"

"No," I deadpanned, putting my fork down so I could properly glare at her.

She shook her head. "Let me finish. I'm not normal, Grayson. My own family hates me. My friends are nonexistent. If I get anything less than an A in school, I lose it. I have panic attacks and I can't handle crowded places. If you don't want to———"

"Shut up, Cupcake. I'm not going anywhere," I said through gritted teeth, picking up my fork and taking a bite. "Eat your French toast," I said, my tone low and barely controlled.

Did she seriously think I'd walk out of here because she liked to keep her things organized? Because she had a few issues?

It would take a whole lot more to scare me off of Nell Watson.

"Oh," she mumbled, focusing once more on the plate in front of her. "Okay."

She chewed a piece of French toast, her eyes still downcast as a slow smile spread across her lips, dimpling her cheek. "Can I ask you something?" she said.

The anger I'd felt at hearing her giving me an 'out' evaporated as soon as her dimple appeared and I felt my own lips stretch into a matching grin.

My heart rate kicked up a couple notches and my throat went dry. "Yeah," I rasped.

She bit her lip, her throat working as she swallowed a laugh. "How in the hell did they screw up French toast?" Her eyes were liquid with laughter as she looked from her plate to me and back again, stabbing the limp piece of toast with her fork and raising it upwards to inspect. "Look at it," she said, stifling a giggle. "It doesn't even look like bread."

I coughed over the chuckle working its way up my throat. "It's really bad, isn't it?"

"So bad," she said, her shoulders shaking as she stopped trying to hold back her laughter. "I think," she swallowed hard, choking on the words, "I think there's something wrong with that milkshake. How is not even pink? It looks nothing like a strawberry milkshake."

"I dare you, Cupcake. I dare you to drink it," I said, laughing lightly as I pushed her milkshake closer to her.

"I'm not sure I'm ready to put my life on the line, Grayson. What do I get if I do it?"

Anything.

"I'll give you another lesson," I said, clearing my throat.

She frowned. "What kind of lesson?"

"Driving my bike."

Her expression cleared and excitement flashed in her eyes. "Deal," she mumbled, swallowing hard and pulling her shake closer to her. "It can't be that bad, right?"

"You tell me," I said, crossing my arms over my chest and watching as her lips came into contact with the straw.

Screwing her eyes shut, she took a drink. "Oh my god," she croaked, her eyes watering as her features twisted with disgust. "Oh my god," she repeated, staring at the shake in front of her in horror. "What is wrong with it?" She gave a helpless chuckle. "It's almost worth it to try it just to see how little it tastes like a strawberry milkshake."

"Yeah, I'm not drinking that," I said, pushing my shake further away when she nudged it closer to me.

"But seriously, you're missing out. You like science. Think of it as a science experiment."

I quirked a brow in her direction, deflecting the drink again. "What makes you think I like science?"

She shrugged. "Don't you?"

"Yeah," I replied, wrapping my hand around the base of the glass she was still trying to push in my direction. "I'm still not drinking this poison."

"Fine," she said, sinking back into her seat and grinning over at me. "But I upheld my end of the bargain and if I live through the night, I fully intend on claiming my winnings."

"I'm not going back on my word, Cupcake," I said, slipping out of the booth and leaving some money on the table. "Let's get out of here." I stuck my hand out to her, palm up, and attempted to ignore the way my heart hammered when she reached out to me and slipped her hand into mine without hesitation.

"Hey!" the waitress said, just as I reached out to grab the door. We both turned around to look at her, and I wondered if I hadn't left enough money. "Do you guys want any of that to-go?"

Nell made an odd choking noise as she shook her head and I bit down on the inside of my cheek hard to keep from laughing. "No, we're good," I managed to say before we bolted out of there.

As soon as the door closed behind us, Nell started laughing and I couldn't stop myself from laughing with her. "Do you think she's ever actually eaten there?"

"Maybe she has no taste buds?" Nell suggested through her laughter.

I pretended to consider it, my mock serious expression ruined by the chuckles that kept escaping. "It's the only reasonable explanation. She seemed genuinely shocked that we didn't eat more."

She laughed again, shaking her head in disbelief. Abruptly, her laughter cut off and her eyes widened as she took in her surroundings. "What time is it?" she asked, tension in her voice.

I shrugged, my humour fading as fast as hers. "Late," I mumbled, wanted to postpone the inevitable, to hold onto the carefree Nell she'd been a second ago, laughter in her eyes and a wide smile on her lips.

"The sun's starting to come up," she said, her white teeth sinking into the soft flesh of her lower lip. "I need to go home."

"Okay. You gonna be in trouble, Cupcake?"

She shrugged, giving me a weak smile. "Probably. I've never done anything like this before. I'm not exactly a rule breaker."

I frowned. "Paige stays out all the time. Why would they care?"

She sighed. "It's different."

"Yeah, she's younger, less trustworthy and a hundred times more likely to end up in jail than you. Are they seriously going to give you a hard time?"

She let out a breath and ran a hand through her tangled hair. "I don't know, Grayson. Let's just go, okay?"

"Fine," I said, grabbing our helmets from the bike's compartment. I handed Nell hers and she strapped it on without a word, her eyes unfocused, her forehead wrinkled.

I couldn't shake the feeling that she was scared, really scared of what she faced when she went back home.

My gaze roved over her features, remembering the bruises that Brian asshole had put on her skin. Were her parents like that? Would they hurt her for going against them?

"Your parents..." I began, my hands clenched into fists at my sides. "Do they...do they hurt you, Nell? If you come home late, are they going to——"

"No!" she said, shaking her head hard and taking a step closer to me. "No, it's not like that." She sighed, her shoulders slumping forward. "They just expect a lot from me, that's all."

The shadows in her eyes told me that wasn't all. That it wasn't even close.

I opened my mouth to argue with her, to get her to explain why it suddenly seemed like the weight of the world was sitting on her shoulders but before I could get a word out, she said, "Please, Grayson. I'm tired. Can we just go?"

I snapped my mouth shut and after a long beat, I turned away from her to swing my leg over the bike. I felt her settle in behind me, her arms wrapping around my waist without hesitation, her front flush with my back. I swallowed hard and took a deep breath, trying to slow my heart rate as I started the motorcycle.

I didn't take the long way to her house and in too short a time, we were there. I stopped at the end of the block, knowing and hating that she wouldn't be asking me to bring her to her driveway this time.

I cut the engine and gritted my teeth when she pulled away from me and dismounted. Blanking my expression, I followed suit and turned to face her, taking my helmet off with one hand while accepting the spare she handed me before hanging them on the handlebars.

"Your jacket," she mumbled, shrugging the leather off before handing it to me.

I nodded, taking it from her and tossing it over the seat of my bike before crossing my arms over my chest, ready for her to walk away without looking back.

Instead, she cocked her head to the side and surprised me. "You're mad at me."

My jaw clenched. "No, I'm not."

Her lips twisted in a wry smile. "Yeah, that was believable."

I let out a short breath, running a hand through my hair in exasperation. "I'm not mad, Nell. I'm just...I'm worried about you. I get that you're nervous about confronting your parents after being out for most of the night but by the way you're acting, I get the feeling that it's more than just nerves. What am I missing here?"

She swallowed hard and looked towards her house. "It's complicated," she said after a moment.

"Yeah, I'm getting that. Why do they treat you so differently than Paige?"

She winced. "Because I have a history of screwing up."

I frowned. "What are you talking about?"

She shook her head slightly, her eyes locking onto mine for a moment before she shot me a smile that didn't reach her eyes. "Nothing."

"It's not nothing," I said through gritted teeth.

She shrugged, her smile fading as she took a step closer to me. "Grayson?"

I blinked down at her, my frustration evaporating as she came even closer, her toes touching mine, her hand reaching out to lay flat on my chest. "Yeah?" I rasped.

"I'm really tired," she replied, her gaze going unfocused as she looked at her hand on my chest, her fingers moving slightly against the fabric of my shirt.

I cleared my throat. "Okay."

"And I think because of that, my impulse control is out the window."

I blinked, not really following. "What?"

She mumbled something that sounded kind of like, "Screw it," and then her arms were wrapped around me, her cheek fitting perfectly where my neck and shoulder meet. "Thank you," she whispered, her voice so soft that if she hadn't been so close to me, I wouldn't have heard it.

By the time my brain managed to function enough to consider hugging her back, I realized that my arms were already around her, holding her securely against me. One of my hands had worked its way up towards her neck, my fingers splayed across the impossibly soft skin exposed at her nape.

I'd never been much for hugging. Maybe it was because my mom hadn't been around when I was growing up, but my dad rarely hugged us and my brother and I had never been the kind of siblings that showed affection like that.

I could probably count the number of genuine hugs I'd given and received in my life and it likely wouldn't take up all my fingers and toes.

This one blew all the other ones out of the water.

I could've stood there all night hugging Nell Watson, feeling her breath rhythmically shift across the skin on my neck, her fingers splayed across my back as if to keep me there.

"I'm glad you came tonight," she whispered and when she pulled back, I had to forcibly stop myself from tightening my grip on her.

"Me too," I rasped.

"See you on Monday," she said before stepping away from me and turning her back.

I watched her walk the block to her house. It wasn't until she'd disappeared inside that my brain started to function properly again.

Once it did, I let out a groan and tilted my head back to look up at the stars. "I'm losing it." I shook my head and stowed the spare helmet in its compartment before putting mine on and climbing onto the bike. "It was just a hug," I mumbled as I started the motorcycle and put it into gear, wondering when it was that Nell Watson had gotten so firmly under my skin.

She winced. "Because I have a history of screwing up."

I frowned. "What are you talking about?"

She shook her head slightly, her eyes locking onto mine for a moment before she shot me a smile that didn't reach her eyes. "Nothing."

"It's not nothing," I said through gritted teeth.

She shrugged, her smile fading as she took a step closer to me. "Grayson?"

I blinked down at her, my frustration evaporating as she came even closer, her toes touching mine, her hand reaching out to lay flat on my chest. "Yeah?" I rasped.

"I'm really tired," she replied, her gaze going unfocused as she looked at her hand on my chest, her fingers moving slightly against the fabric of my shirt.

I cleared my throat. "Okay."

"And I think because of that, my impulse control is out the window."

I blinked, not really following. "What?"

She mumbled something that sounded kind of like, "Screw it," and then her arms were wrapped around me, her cheek fitting perfectly where my neck and shoulder meet. "Thank you," she whispered, her voice so soft that if she hadn't been so close to me, I wouldn't have heard it.

By the time my brain managed to function enough to consider hugging her back, I realized that my arms were already around her, holding her securely against me. One of my hands had worked its way up towards her neck, my fingers splayed across the impossibly soft skin exposed at her nape.

I'd never been much for hugging. Maybe it was because my mom hadn't been around when I was growing up, but my dad rarely hugged us and my brother and I had never been the kind of siblings that showed affection like that.

I could probably count the number of genuine hugs I'd given and received in my life and it likely wouldn't take up all my fingers and toes.

This one blew all the other ones out of the water.

I could've stood there all night hugging Nell Watson, feeling her breath rhythmically shift across the skin on my neck, her fingers splayed across my back as if to keep me there.

"I'm glad you came tonight," she whispered and when she pulled back, I had to forcibly stop myself from tightening my grip on her.

"Me too," I rasped.

"See you on Monday," she said before stepping away from me and turning her back.

I watched her walk the block to her house. It wasn't until she'd disappeared inside that my brain started to function properly again.

Once it did, I let out a groan and tilted my head back to look up at the stars. "I'm losing it." I shook my head and stowed the spare helmet in its compartment before putting mine on and climbing onto the bike. "It was just a hug," I mumbled as I started the motorcycle and put it into gear, wondering when it was that Nell Watson had gotten so firmly under my skin.